JAY E. ADAMS
The Biblical View of

Self-Esteem

Self-Love

Self-Image

HARVEST HOUSE PUBLISHERS
Eugene, Oregon 97402

Except where otherwise indicated, all Scripture quotations in this book are taken from the New American Standard Bible, © The Lockman Foundation 1960, 1962, 1963, 1968, 1971, 1972, 1973, 1975, 1977. Used by permission.

Verses marked KJV are taken from the King James Version of the Bible.

THE BIBLICAL VIEW OF SELF-ESTEEM, SELF-LOVE & SELF-IMAGE

Copyright © 1986 by Harvest House Publishers
Eugene, Oregon 97402

Library of Congress Catalog Card Number 86-080705
ISBN 0-89081-553-4

Printed in the United States of America.

PREFACE

During the last 15 years we have seen the rise of a powerful and influential movement within the church. You can easily identify it by observing the use of one or more of the several closely related labels with which it is intimately associated: self-image, self-esteem, self-worth, and self-love. The one common denominator, regardless of the nomenclature used by any particular advocate of this movement, is the emphasis on self. Such persons regularly speak and write about "coming to a high view of self," "feeling good about yourself," "gaining a sense of personal value and worth," and the like. Whatever their differences, the one enemy against which they are unitedly fighting is *low self-esteem*.

We cannot judge the motivations or intentions of those who take differing points of view on this topic. Some make only passing reference to self-image or self-esteem, while others incorporate not only the terminology but the entire philosophy into their understanding of truth. Still others shun the movement and forthrightly call it unbiblical.

The self-esteem influence has so pervaded our society that it is no longer perceived as anything but the most familiar and acceptable way of thinking. It will be our task in this book to understand and evaluate this movement in order to determine whether it is biblical or not and to determine how Christians should relate to it. In addition, we must find what impact it is having on the ministry, congregations, parents, children, teachers, and Christian schools.

Is this movement true? False? Good? Bad? Innocuous? Dangerous? Partly one or partly the other? If it is a threat to the faith, how shall we counter it? It is to these and similar questions that I shall address myself in this book, for all of us as Christians need to clearly perceive the truth and conform our lives to it.

—Jay E. Adams

CONTENTS

What's Going On?

My first concern is to help you get an accurate picture of how widespread and far-reaching the self-esteem movement is. I want you to see that it is not simply a passing fad to be quickly replaced by the next one. It has been coming on slowly for a long time, but now that it is here, it has suddenly assumed proportions far greater than anyone could have predicted and has attained so large a place in the thinking of many Christian leaders that we can be sure that its teachings will have impact on the church not only in this generation but in the next as well. And it is important to note that this phenomenon is not something isolated within the church but is broadly accepted and propagated in non-Christian circles as well. Indeed, one of the surprising peculiarities of the situation is that, unlike many other emphases currently found in society in general, liberals, nonbelievers, and Bible-believing Christians alike are caught up in the self-esteem movement. It is one of those few ideologically based movements in which one may find friend and foe alike.

Let's take a look, then, at some of the things that have been happening and that are being said.

In the *Banner*, August 13, 1984, it was reported that—

> In Grand Rapids 500 Christian school children from the fourth and fifth grades were given a week's training in "how to recognize" their "true worth." They wrote essays on why they liked themselves (or didn't), they acted out a skit called "A Pat on the Back," and were told "feel good about yourselves."

It is hardly necessary to point out that this approach is based on a point of view toward those children that, if followed up consistently by similar teaching and treatment in the Christian schools of Grand Rapids, should have quite an influence on them as well as on their teachers. But what will be the impact of such teaching? Will it be for the good of those children and their schools, or will it harm them? What will it do to teaching? And . . . what will it do to tomorrow's church when a generation of children so taught will take over?

This matter is vitally important, and its consequences in society are going to be significant. The State of California has been considering setting up a commission to study self-esteem (to the tune of 750,000 dollars annually) with a view to reducing crime through raising the self-image of otherwise potential criminal types.[1] If the teachings and practices of the self-worth movement can help Christian schoolchildren and potential criminals, no wonder such views have become so widespread! This is a large order; what can the self-image approach *not* do?

Not much, according to the enthusiastic writers who proclaim the self-esteem dogma. According to one Christian author, whose book on self-esteem was sent free to nearly every pastor in America, the answer to that question certainly would be "Very little!" In his book he says, "I contend that this unfulfilled need for self-esteem underlies every act."[2] That's quite a claim! If it is true, proper self-esteem is the secret to life and most of its problems. But isn't that going a bit far? Not according to the best-selling book *Self-Esteem: The New Reformation*, which states, "Self-esteem is . . . the single, greatest need facing the human race today,"[3] or according to one of the leading Christian psychologists, who says, "If I could write a prescription for the women of the world, I would provide each one of them with a healthy dose of self-esteem and personal worth. . . . I have no doubt that this is their greatest need."[4]

In a recent issue of the *Ladies Home Journal,* women are assured that "feeling good about ourselves may, in fact, be the cornerstone of our total well-being."[5] Since they think this is likely, the writers of the article logically give the following advice: "Take positive steps to enhance" your "self-esteem."[6] The advice is not uncommon either within or without the church—for women or for men.

But, while we are speaking of women, listen to this author from one of the most conservative, fundamentalist schools in the country:

> A mother's second area of responsibility
> during pregnancy is in meeting the psycho-
> logical needs of her baby. The most basic
> psychological need of the baby in the womb is
> to have a mother who has a positive self-
> concept or self-esteem. The emotional cli-
> mate during pregnancy is established by the
> mother's view of herself.[7]

Plainly, if these writers are correct, women especially must come to grips with this matter of self-worth.
Not only their own well-being but the welfare of the
children they carry depends on it.

The author whom I last quoted, who so strongly lays
self-esteem responsibility on pregnant women, makes
this further connection: "Mothers who choose to
obtain abortions do so because of too little self-esteem,
not too much."[8] He is not alone in this notion. Walter
Trobisch wrote, "I wonder whether one of the deepest
roots of the abortion problem does not lie here. . . .
Can an expectant mother who wishes to abort her child
really love herself?"[9]

Is self-esteem really so important that it can be a
matter of life or death? Absolutely, say the self-worth
proponents. A recent article in the *Christian School
and Home* categorically asserted that—

> The basic psychological cause of any suicide
> is that the individual has lost any hope of find-
> ing any meaning in this present life. Loss of
> hope, of love, or of self-esteem in this present
> life is the foundation. . . [10]

James Dobson agrees: "...lack of self-esteem can actually extinguish the desire to go on living."[11]

Right or wrong, at least that's what one school superintendent thought. Taking his life by shooting himself through the heart with a .357 magnum, Frederick Holliday, Cleveland's first black school superintendent, left a note in which he explained his action. Among other things he said:

> I have had great success as a schoolman and a leader.... As of the moment, it appears that my last piece of dignity is being stripped.[12]

It seems that two board members were accusing Holliday of being "too cozy" with the white business community. The city council president said that "Holliday felt 'his personal integrity was on the line.'"[13]

In other words, his self-worth, or self-esteem, was being challenged.

If you think that this is an isolated case and that people are not taking this self-esteem teaching seriously enough to make it a matter of their life and death, then listen to the suicide note left behind by 18-year-old Wanda Williams:

> Nothing happened last year to make life worth while. A year ago exactly I made a sort of bargain with God or fate, and this is my part of the bargain. I agreed that if something didn't happen last year—to make life worth living and make me somebody, that at the end of the year I would quit living. That wasn't

asking too much, but I didn't get it. Please
don't think this is something brought on by
late events. Suicide is a coward's way out, so
I am a coward. I just don't have the courage
to go on just existing.[14]

Did you get those words—"to make life worth
living. . . to make me somebody"? That's what Wanda
wanted—to be known as somebody. Those are self-
esteem statements. As a matter of fact, the presence
of the words "You're somebody" in any talk or writing is a telltale sign of self-worth teaching; they run
all through certain strands of the self-worth literature.
For example, in one booklet published and distributed
widely by a Christian publishing house, the writer says,
"You have to think that you are somebody" if you
want to maintain good mental health.[15] Other Christian writers have published a book indicating a similar theme—for example, *The Sensation of Being
Somebody* and *You're Someone Special.* In the first,
the writer calls the good feelings that come from self-
worth "somebody feelings."[16]
Wanda was a girl who concluded that she was a
nobody and, exactly one year later because "God or
fate" didn't make her a somebody, went out and
hanged herself! From all that the self-esteem proponents espouse, we could reach only one conclusion
about the cause of her suicide: The problem was that
her self-esteem needs were not met. In his reflec-
tions on her suicide in his book *Why We Act That
Way,* Miller sees it differently: "It's a pity someone
didn't tell that young 18-year-old girl that no one ever
finds life worth living. He makes it worth living by

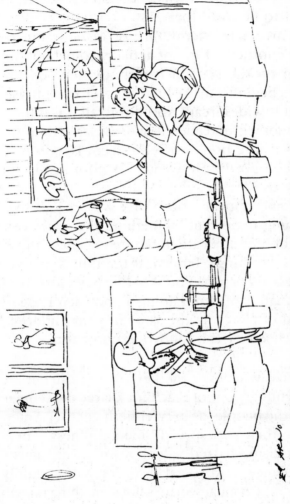

"I don't like *myself*, and Peter doesn't like *himself*, but we do like each other."

surrendering himself up to something that is worth
living for. God lives up to His end of the bargain, He
has filled this world with ideas, ideals, and causes that
cry out to be lived for.''[17]

In a cartoon by Victor, *Funny Business,* one person
says to another, ''I'm not actually somebody myself,
but I'm on the staff of somebody.'' When the car-
toonists begin to make fun of a word or phrase, you
know it is widespread! Apropos to all this is the warning of another fundamentalist Christian writer, the sub-
title of whose book on self-esteem is *You're Better
Than You Think*. He wrote, ''A poor self-image can
destroy us.''[18]

It would appear, then, that we are dealing with
something important, something that can even be a
matter of life and death, if we are to believe those who
tell us such things. Indeed, if the things you've been
reading are correct, you'd better pay close attention
to the matter of maintaining a good self-image yourself and of fostering the same in your children. This
is evidenced by the following quotation:

> Thus, whenever the keys to self-esteem are
> seemingly out of reach for a large percentage
> of the people, as in twentieth-century Amer-
> ica, then widespread ''mental illness,'' neu-
> roticism, hatred, alcoholism, drug abuse,
> violence, and social disorder will certainly
> occur. Personal worth is not something human
> beings are free to take or leave. We must have
> it and when it is unattainable, everybody
> suffers.[19]

If this view is correct, think of how important proper self-worth teaching in the church could be. This issue, as the self-image people claim, should be of significance to individual Christians, to Christian parents, to preachers, to Christian schoolteachers—in fact, to all of us. The responsibility for understanding and for proper action on our part is enormous!

In the next chapter we shall try to understand a bit more about this movement.

2

A Demand for Change

I have asserted that the self-worth, self-esteem movement cannot be ignored. It is of importance. If it is correct, we must all change our ways—in the home, in the church, and in the school. The leaders of the movement recognize this fact and loudly call for such change. Should we heed their call?

Parents are being told to train and discipline their children differently. A Christian theologian, a professor of systematic theology, writes on the subject of self-image:

> Parents should also handle disciplinary problems in such a way as not to damage a child's positive self-image.[1]

This theme is echoed and reechoed relentlessly throughout self-esteem literature. The call is a call for change. Heretofore parents thought little or nothing about such matters. Now, they are told, your child's self-image is all-important.

What these leaders are saying implies all sorts of new considerations for discipline in the home and in the Christian school, many of which they recommend we garner from such psychologists as Tom Gordon, Haim Ginott, and Percival Symonds, the last of whom is quoted favorably as saying:

> Parents and teachers should be extremely sensitive to the attitude they express toward children. . . . Children respond not only to what is said to them and about them but also to the attitudes, gestures and subtle shades of expression that indicate how parents and teachers feel.[2]

The self-esteem advocates place a heavy burden on parents—how they must always be deeply cognizant of gestures and subtle shades of facial expressions! If they aren't, all sorts of horrible things are likely to happen to their children. This new teaching gives us quite a different view of children, doesn't it? No longer can we think of them as those bouncy, resilient little creatures that we once thought they were. They are to be considered extremely sensitive, fragile, and easily warped by the most subtle shades of parental miscues. That's something to think about.

Another Christian writer discusses how parents and teachers must *build* a child's self-esteem. Here we see that there is also *positive work* that we must do. It is not enough to be careful not to hinder the growth of self-worth, but we must actively promote it in our children. She writes, "Parents and teachers need to evaluate the messages that they are sending to their children."[3] In discussing the matter of punishing a child in public she says, "Discipline should be a private matter," and then gives this reason: "to help a child retain his dignity."[4]

The child is said to possess dignity. It is that reason in particular to which I call your attention. She continues:

> God has entrusted you to convey a sense of self-worth to a few of His little ones. You're called to invest time, energy, patience, sensitivity and often creative thinking.[5]

This is a new concept to many parents and teachers. Clearly this movement is demanding change, change that is radical and time-consuming. It is change that places huge amounts of new responsibility for the welfare of children upon the shoulders of parents and every other adult who comes into contact with children. It makes one wonder if he is able to create and maintain the optimum environment in his home, and whether he should ever allow his child out of the house. Surely he cannot expect other people to cater to his child with such care and delicacy as seems to be demanded.

If this way of thinking is right, and it is our God-given task to convey a sense of self-worth to children, then we have a much larger job on our hands in bringing up children than our parents ever envisioned when they raised us. But if life and death, joy and suicide, fulfillment in life and abortion are the things

that hang in the balance, then we *must* buy into the
new teaching!

But you have heard only the half of it; the self-esteem
movement bites even more deeply. It demands changes
in our churches—in our worship and preaching. One
seminary professor, who is a staunch advocate of the
self-worth movement, had this to say:

> Fortunately, in the hymnal presently used in
> our church the last line [of Beneath the Cross
> of Jesus] has been changed [from "my own
> worthlessness"] to "And my unworthiness."
> I quite agree that we are unworthy; I do not
> believe that it accords with biblical teaching
> to say that we are worthless.[6]

He criticizes Issac Watts' famous hymn *Alas, and
Did My Savior Bleed?* when it speaks of "such a worm
as I." He comments that the "hymn could convey to
many people a quite unflattering self-image."[7]

This seems to be a strange argument on the face of
it. Since when does the Bible indicate that God is in
the business of flattering sinners? Even today's songs
are beginning to carry the new self-esteem message.
Listen to this line from verse 3 of the song *They'll
Know We Are Christians:* ". . . and we'll guard each
man's dignity and save each man's pride." Such sen-
timents could never have been penned by the author
of *When I Survey the Wondrous Cross*, which contains
the words "and pour contempt on all my pride," or
by the writer of *Amazing Grace,* in which is found
the line, "that saved a wretch like me." Surely there

is a change not only that is to come but that has already come!

Robert Schuller, who is a foremost propagator of the self-esteem movement, at least has the courage and the insight to see the implications of the principles of the new movement. Unlike most others in the church who have accepted them, he does not hesitate to carry those principles to their logical extreme. If it is a good and proper thing to follow the ways of self-worth, then Schuller's thesis is correct: We need nothing short of a new reformation. He rightly sees that anything less than this will fall short of the ends advocated by the new movement. Theology itself will be affected.

Indeed, Schuller calls for a "New Reformation," dubbing the sixteenth-century movement under Luther and Calvin a "reactionary movement" because it emphasized the fact that men are sinners. Schuller writes, "Once a person believes he is an 'unworthy sinner,' it is doubtful if he can honestly accept the saving grace God offers in Christ."[8] Instead, he tells us, the New Reformation will focus on "the sacred right of every person to self-esteem."[9] His rationale is as follows:

> If you want to know why Schuller smiles on television; if you want to know why I make people laugh once in a while, I'm giving them sounds and strokes, sounds and strokes [like you would a baby]. It's strategy. People who don't trust need to be stroked. People are born with a negative self-image. Because they do not trust, they cannot trust God.[10]

If Schuller is right, evangelism must change. We must not tell people that they are sinners who need Jesus Christ as a Savior, convincing them of their sin and rebellion toward a holy God. We do not talk of hell and warn of the terrible, eternal consequences of rejecting the offer of salvation; no, we must stroke men and women into the faith. That *is* a change! A very large one!

But that is not all. Schuller has an even larger concept in mind:

> A theology of self-esteem also produces a
> theology . . . of social ethics, and a theology
> of economics; and these produce a theology
> of government. It all rises from one founda-
> tion: the dignity of the person who was
> created in the image of God.[11]

Certainly he is right if the new teachings are correct: You cannot have a panacea that does not affect everything. The self-worth doctrines demand sweeping change in theology as well as in all else.

Even depression must be handled in a manner consistent with self-worth teaching. Dr. Wayne Colwell, teaching at the Rosemead School of Psychology, told his class, "Depression always has a loss of self-esteem in the foreground. . . . Be slow to direct a depressed person to the Scriptures. . . *no preaching.* I would recommend a recess from church if there is *preaching* done in the church."[12]

Remember what the theologians used to say? Here is a theologian-hymnwriter from the past:

> In all unbelief there are two things—a good opinion of self and a bad opinion of God. So long as these things exist, it is impossible for an inquirer to find rest. His good opinion of himself makes him think it quite possible to win God's favor by his own religious performances. . . . The object of the Holy Spirit's work, in convicting of sin, is to alter the sinner's opinion of himself, and so to reduce his estimate of his own character that he shall think of himself as God does. . . .[13]

Clearly those words teach just the opposite of what self-esteem advocates are saying. Bonar's understanding of Scripture leads him to believe that people have too much self-esteem, and that this in turn hinders them from trusting Christ as Savior. He sees the work of the Holy Spirit in evangelism as destroying this high opinion that the sinner has of himself. You can't have it both ways; either the old view must be replaced or the new view must be rejected. They are irrevocably incompatible.

Bonar continues:

> It takes a great deal to destroy a man's good opinion of himself, and even after he has lost his good opinion of his works, he retains a good opinion of his heart; and even after he has lost that, he holds fast his good opinion of his religious duties. . . .[14]

One does not have to go as far back as Bonar's day for such teaching. As recently as 30 years ago it was

"I once tried to be somebody
but it just wasn't me!"

not uncommon to pick up books that spoke of "helping persons escape self-love" so that they might "experience outgoing, altruistic love of the brethren."[15]

Finally, on this point, consider one more brief quotation:

> All these difficulties of yours have their root
> in the self-esteem of our natures, which makes
> us refuse to be counted altogether sinners. . . .
> The Holy Spirit's work in convincing you of
> sin is to make you dissatisfied with yourself.[16]

Certainly this older, standard evangelical view of man and his problem, and the New Reformation, self-esteem views are at odds. Contrast the words of a noted Christian author:

> The individual who has a good self-image
> feels worthwhile. He feels good about himself
> and likes himself. He accepts both his positive
> qualities and his weaknesses.[17]

There is a new wind blowing through the church today. It demands change—a change of viewpoint, belief, and approach. Is it true or is it false? You must decide; you cannot go both east and west at the same time; man's problem cannot be at the same time too little and too much self-esteem. In order to help you come to this decision, in the next chapter I shall explore the origins of this movement and more of its teachings.

What Brought This On? 3

You may be wondering how the new movement made its way into the Christian church, what its origins are, and what its central tenets are. Plainly it is saying that self-esteem—a good self-image—is central to success in life, and, according to some, even in death. These large claims and the enormous amounts of concomitant responsibilities that they imply must be understood in terms of their theoretical basis and then compared and contrasted with biblical presuppositions, principles, and practices.

Does the New Reformation doctrine come from the Bible? If not, where did it originate? Is it compatible with biblical thinking?

A leading evangelical psychologist, who vigorously promotes self-worth teaching, explains that—

> Under the influence of humanistic psychologists like Carl Rogers and Abraham Maslow,

many of us Christians have begun to see our
need for self-love and self-esteem.[1]

This statement plainly points to a source outside
the church and outside the Bible. The self-love, self-
worth movement did not originate out of new exeget-
ical and theological study; it was accommodated and
incorporated into the teaching of the church. Its
fundamental concepts were hammered out elsewhere.
While it originated in the ranks of the so-called "third
force" psychologists like those mentioned above, its
theoretical base goes back to Alfred Adler. Christian
psychologists and psychiatrists brought in this teaching
from *outside* the church.

Certainly, everything that a psychologist has to say
is not necessarily incorrect; if he tells us that the sky
is up and the dirt is down we accept his words as true.
But, over the couple of generations that modern
psychologists have been at it, they have offered so
many panaceas for the world's problems (Freudianism,
I'm OK, You're OK thinking, and the like) which in
the long run have failed to do much good and may have
added to the hurts of our world that we can hardly
be blamed for being wary of this latest offering with
its global claims.

Let us approach the new movement cautiously. Even
though the teaching of self-esteem doctrine contradicts
traditional, evangelical Protestant positions, and even
though it originated in the camp of "humanistic psychologists," the so-called Christian psychologists
assure us that "this is a good and necessary focus."[2]
Are they correct? Are these assurances well-founded?

How can it be that new teaching, coming from

humanists, which demands fundamental change in our thinking and our relationships to one another, would be a "good" and even "necessary" focus for us? Everywhere a Christian turns these days he is told that "all truth is God's truth." This is the answer that either in this sloganized form or otherwise is given. Even "humanistic" psychologists, we are assured, may come up with truth. It does not matter that Adler and Maslow were humanists; if they stumbled across truth, so be it. We must accept truth no matter where it comes from.

But the reassurance doesn't help very much, since we also know that *all error is the devil's error.* We must still distinguish between what is truth from God and what is error from the devil. We need more than slogans—they will not help. What we need is a standard against which to compare various views to determine whether they are true or false. That standard can be none other than the Bible, God's inerrant and infallible standard for faith and life. In the end we shall know whether to welcome or reject the new movement, with its large claims and insistent demands of fundamental changes of belief and practice, only as we test it against Scripture itself. This we shall do at a later point, but for now we shall simply try to understand the movement.

We cannot cover everything about the origins and teachings of the self-love, self-worth movements, and to attempt to do so here would be unprofitable. What you need to know is its inner dynamics as its founders have set them forth.

Abraham Maslow is the key figure involved. While he was not the originator of the movement, surely

© 1985 United Feature Syndicate, Inc.

more than any one other person he has given it form and shape as a movement and sold it to the American public. During his days in New York City he attended Friday night seminars in Alfred Adler's home and had many talks with him. He also sought out persons like Eric Fromm and Karen Horney (from whom most of the fragile-child teaching that we have been hearing for more than a generation stems). It was Adler's fundamental view that a person may realize fulfillment and satisfaction only when his needs for security and significance are met. Maslow took this idea, reshaped and amplified it, and then sold it under the heading of self-actualization. Many of the ideas about children that I have already introduced you to in previous chapters seem to have been adapted from Horney.

Maslow was concerned (rightly) about the fact that most theoreticians had developed their concepts of human functioning from cases met in counseling. While there are probably some things wrong with everyone, Maslow thought that the study of man should not proceed from the study of failures, persons having great difficulties, etc. So he set out to study those who were making it, really making it in life—self-actualized persons, as he eventually came to call them. After a thorough study of these persons, he determined that there were 30 or more characteristics that are common to such persons. But he also noted that these self-actualized persons, who could love and reach out beyond themselves to others, were rare finds. Maslow concluded that there are not more self-actualized persons because most persons have not had their needs satisfied at lower levels and consequently are unable to satisfy their need for self-actualization.

This whole phenomenon he envisioned as a "hierachy of needs." This hierachy could be visualized as a pyramid, with each layer resting on and dependent upon the satisfaction of the needs at the level beneath it. Physical needs, such as food, clothing, and shelter, come first. Higher concerns are of little interest when those needs are not met. When the physical needs are met, one becomes concerned about safety and security needs. Only when these are met does he interest himself in love and belongingness needs. Those taken care of (of course for many people they never are), he focuses on self-esteem. It is at this point that many Americans are stuck in the upward progression of concerns today.

Blended together with Adler's earlier, simpler need theory—that everyone needs to have security and significance—the pyramid might look something like the one on the following page.

The correspondence between Adler's and Maslow's need theories is striking when placed together on the pyramid, as I have done.

Perhaps it will become intelligible to you from looking at the chart why many Christians who accept Maslow's formulation say that to love God and to love other people (the sum of the commandments and, for that matter, the entire Scriptures) is not possible for a person until all his other needs have been met. Reaching out to other persons is a self-actualization activity that depends upon the fulfillment of needs at all lower levels.

Note, also, that even at this highest level the actions of a self-actualized person are still *self*-actualizing. That is to say, they are done to meet needs within the

HIERARCHY OF NEEDS

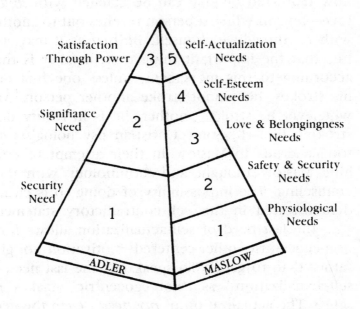

Satisfaction Through Power 3
Self-Actualization Needs 5

4 Self-Esteem Needs

Signifiance Need 2
Love & Belongingness Needs 3

Safety & Security Needs 2

Security Need 1
Physiological Needs 1

ADLER   MASLOW

The correspondence between Adler's and Maslow's need theories is striking when placed together as I have done.

person himself; they are not disinterested or altruistic, since they do not take place for the benefit of another person. God or man is loved *in order to satisfy the needs of the one doing the loving.* One wonders how that kind of love can be equated with *agape* love—love in which a person reaches out to another with no thought of himself. Be that as it may, notice that the important thing to remember is that, according to this movement, unless one first gets his strokes, he cannot stroke another person. And whenever he strokes another, he is in reality only stroking himself. Some Christian psychologists are too generous to Maslow in their attempt to combine Maslow thought and terminology with their counseling. The impossibility of doing so is clearly demonstrated in this self-contradictory statement: "...the last need of self-actualization allows for a non-egocentric other-centered motivation to give rather than to get."[3] To speak of "the last need of *self*-actualization" as "non-egocentric" makes no sense. The actualization of *my need*—even the need to give—is clearly egocentric in motivation.

One widely read Christian says:

> Self love is thus the prerequisite and the criterion for our conduct towards our neighbor... without self-love there can be no love for others.... You cannot love neighbor, you cannot love God unless you first love yourself.[4]

In other words, one's own self-esteem needs (the

layer in the pyramid with which this book is concerned) must first be met before he is able to meet his need to love another person. Neither the first nor the second great commandments of God can be obeyed until a person first loves himself!

Captain has this to say:

> Actually, our ability to love God and to love our neighbor is limited by our ability to love ourselves. We cannot love God more than we love our neighbor and we cannot love our neighbor more than we love ourselves.[5]

Another author wrote:

> People who have poor self-image, who fail to realize their own self-worth, who are always belittling themselves, these people usually have difficulty in loving others properly.[6]

He goes so far as to reverse the biblical command, saying:

> So love yourself, Christian, as you should love others.[7]

This writer claims that people with inadequate self-worth "usually have difficulty in loving others." Another Christian leader has no time for such qualified statements. He says flatly, "Without self-love there can be no love for others."[8] He sets up a paradigm:

> We are unable to love others because we have not learned to love others.
>
> We cannot learn to love ourselves because we are not loved by others or are unable to accept their love.
>
> We are not loved by others because we are unable to love them or we love them only "out of duty."
>
> We are unable to love them because we have not learned to love ourselves.[9]

He paints a vicious circle in which many people become hopelessly caught because there is no one to unwind the circle from the outside. This sort of reasoning tempts one to ask whether Jesus' love to others depended on their prior love for Him.

Not all self-love-movement advocates believe to the same degree everything promoted by the movement. However, without realizing it, those who speak even offhandedly about these "self" concepts are identifying with a way of thinking that has profound implications. It is clear that the new self-love-movement advocate in the church

1. believes firmly (although perhaps unwittingly) in Maslow's pyramid of needs; and

2. believes that love for God and other people rests on satisfaction at the levels below.

But just to make sure that such thinking is an essential part of the entire movement, listen carefully to this Christian who is a psychologist:

> If no one loves us, how will we ever know our value and significance? If we are to have that attitude toward ourselves, we must be esteemed and valued. This means we can never have a positive self-image apart from other people. In our early life, we cannot know love unless our parents love us. And as we grow older, we continue to need to have other people love us. . . . [10]

If it is true that we cannot know the love of God or other people unless we ourselves have been adequately loved, there are many implications growing out of this fact, some of which we have encountered already. As we have seen, there are those who think that needs represented at various levels of the pyramid go back to the womb!

But all of this sounds somewhat abstract. How does this work out in practice? The following is a slice of a counseling case that demonstrates the theory in actual practice:

> Midge is a 23-year-old, single working girl. She is a graduate of a Bible college where she is employed as a secretary. On her Personal Data Inventory [the intake sheet used at The Christian Counseling and Educational Foundation and by many nouthetic counselors] she describes herself as "often blue, shy and

lonely." She also adds, *"I'm a nothing,"* and
"I feel inferior." She says that she prays often
but reads her Bible only occasionally.

As she sees it, this is the main problem: *"My
self-concept is just absolutely zero.* That may
surprise you, but it is. *My whole life has been
a big, fat zero. Nobody notices me, nobody
likes me and nobody cares about me.* I may
as well be dead. *I feel so inadequate.* Even
when I pray I can't find any relief. *Probably
the Lord doesn't even like me.* But He is the
One who made me this way, so maybe He
does."[11]

Note well the self-esteem language in which Midge
expresses herself. While the tenets of the new movement thoroughly undergird her entire evaluation of her
situation, the phrases that I have italicized especially
stand out as self-love, self-worth expressions. From this
case, you can see that she has been diligently taught
the doctrines of self-image and self-worth: Other
people have not done as they should to her, so she has
little or no sense of self-worth and is stuck in a
meaningless and pitiful life. Obviously, in this condition, dependent upon other people for ego strength,
she has no thought of reaching out to others. Even God
has let her down. Her problems stem from the failures
of others to meet her needs.

This idea that a person cannot reach out to others
in love until he learns to love himself occurs and
reoccurs in Christian literature. Speaking of a 20-
year-old who had attempted suicide a third time, the

Christian writer who evaluated his situation claims that—

> He had virtually no self-image, thinking very little of himself and therefore wishing to end what he thought to be a useless life . . . what he termed to be "bad experiences" kept him from loving himself and from loving others.[12]

To pick just one more out of hundreds of such statements:

> Modern psychology has finally come to the conclusion that the great driving force of all human behavior is needs. A child is born with needs; to be loved, to be accepted, to be thought important. He's got to have it or he won't live![13]

Growing out of this kind of thinking is one large implication for theology and its practical expression in everyday life: If what self-image theorists say is true and if Midge is right—man cannot be held responsible to obey God's commands to love himself and his neighbor if he did not first receive the proper strokes himself.

This all-important issue will be considered later on, but here are some principal facts gleaned so far:

1. The self-love movement that was begun by humanistic psychologists has already had a significant impact on the church.
2. This movement confronts old beliefs and

practices, challenging them and demanding changes.

3. You cannot simply "add" the insights of this new teaching to your set of existing Christian beliefs; if you add them, you must modify or subtract many of the beliefs you already hold. You cannot have it both ways. You must choose between traditional, evangelical views and the "New Reformation."

4. You are choosing between two divergent views of man, his problem, and how to solve it.

In the chapters that follow, I shall try to help you make that choice.

4

Let's Test It Biblically

In the previous chapters I have tried to present an overview of the new self-esteem movement. I quoted from the writings of some of its leading proponents, chiefly those from conservative, Bible-believing circles. I pointed out how sweeping the implications of its teachings and practices are, so sweeping that some proponents are calling it a "New Reformation" that will correct the excesses and errors of the sixteenth-century Reformation. Even though most proponents do not use such terminology or understand all its implications, it is perfectly clear that they are asking for nothing less than this.

I indicated that the church already has been strongly affected by self-esteem thrusts which seem to have penetrated every conceivable area of ministry. Self-esteem teachers, on every hand, are confronting cherished beliefs, replacing our childrearing practices with new ones, rewriting our hymnbooks, and demanding change in our preaching. I concluded by insisting that the new views are not something you can add to your Christian repertoire, but which, if accepted, must *replace* much of what you once believed. As parents, teachers, and pastors, all that you do will be radically affected.

If the self-worth advocates are right, then for the sake of our children, for the welfare of the church, and for our own sakes (preeminently this!) we must be willing to change. We cannot hold on to past views because they are comfortable or cherished. The only question that may rightfully concern us, according to God's Word, is whether what they say is correct. I am not a hidebound conservative who will hold on to beliefs or practices because "we have always done it that way." My entire ministry has been devoted to innovation and change. When I have concluded that old ways were unbiblical, I have been among the first to try to change them. I have been listening carefully to what the self-image people are saying. If they are right, we all must be willing to make large changes. We dare not hold to tradition for tradition's sake. But, on the other hand, if the clock has been moved forward erroneously, we must set it back.

In the first three chapters I tried to do as little evaluating as possible. I did raise some questions as we went along, and on occasion I promised that we would take a hard look at the new movement from a biblical perspective. It is now time to begin to do so.

Let's start where we left off—by reconsidering Maslow's hierarchy of needs. In Maslow's construct of the human being, unless his needs are met at lower levels, higher-level activity cannot be expected from him. As Crabb puts it:

The essential factor in Maslow's theory is
that people are not motivated to meet the
"higher" needs until the "lower" or more
basic ones are met.[1]

This means, among other things, that man cannot
be held responsible for obedience to the biblical commands to love God and his neighbor if he has been
deprived of lower-level satisfactions that are requisite
for obedience.

But nowhere in the entire Bible is any such idea
suggested, let alone set forth as a principle for life. We
simply do not find any statements in either the Old
or New Testaments even hinting that Christians must
have other people meet their basic needs in order to
make it possible for them to obey God's commandments. Especially do we fail to find anything about a
supposed "need to love one's self" as a prerequisite
for loving others. Nothing in the Scriptures even
approximates this.

What we *do* discover when we study the question
of "needs" in the Bible is not a plethora of foundational and subsidiary needs piled up at various levels
but the deliniation of the barest minimum of such
needs:

If we have food and covering, with these we
shall be content. (1 Timothy 6:8).

There you have material needs that seem to approximate Maslow's bottommost level. But even that
identification is too easy and superficial. At a still
more foundational level, unknown to either Adler or

Maslow, we must consider these words of Jesus:

> Only a few things are necessary, really only
> one (Luke 10:42).

That one essential need is to hear Him and believe His Word, as Mary did. Rather than multiply needs, biblical writers seem to go to great lengths to deny any such accumulation. Jesus, in reducing needs to their barest minimum, not only makes the point that "a person can't sustain life on bread alone," but here in Luke 10:42 indicates that the only life which is absolutely essential is the life that is sustained by "every word that proceeds out of the mouth of God."[2]

What Jesus is telling Martha is that in any choice between food for the body and food for the soul, the latter must always take precedence because it alone is absolutely essential. He says, "Mary has chosen the good part, *which shall not be taken away from her*" (Luke 10:42). It is better because it is everlasting!

We shall all die someday, and even food and clothing will mean nothing to us then. Whether we have fed on the life-giving Words of Christ, however, will be of the utmost importance.

Some Christian psychologists are confusing the church with such statements as the following:

> People have one basic personal need which
> requires two kinds of input for its satisfaction.
> The most basic need is a sense of personal
> worth, an acceptance of oneself as a whole,
> real person.[3]

There is absolutely no biblical basis for any such statement. Indeed, following the Adler-Maslow line too closely here leads Crabb to contradict Jesus' words: "There is only one real need"(Luke 10:42). The real need of which He spoke was not the "need" for a sense of personal worth or for the acceptance of oneself as a whole, real person. It was the need for Himself and His Word.

Because their counseling system is so tightly tied to Adler at this point, such Christian psychologists think this one "most basic need" is satisfied by gaining significance and security. Unlike Adler, however, they say that significance and security may be found only in Christ. This confusion of what is basic and what is not is occasioned by an unfortunate dependence upon Adlerian concepts.

Obviously we are faced with a choice here. Shall we continue to recognize the need theory of the Bible as the basis for our understanding of humanity, or shall we abandon it for the speculations of modern psychologists?

In Matthew 6 Jesus contrasts the "Gentile" (or pagan) philosophy of life with the Christian approach. He observes that the pagan zealously seeks security in "things" (a prominent term in the chapter) that he thinks he "needs." He even mentions as His prime example what Maslow and Adler consider to be the two bottom level needs: food and clothing! Yet rather than concluding that these needs are essential to higher-level activity (as fundamental and basic as they may be thought to be), Jesus turns everything around and stands Maslow's pyramid on its apex:

> Seek first His kingdom and His righteousness,
> and all these things shall be added to you (Mat-
> thew 6:33).

Jesus is saying that the so-called "basic things" that are needed should not be of prime concern in life. They are not basic after all; they are but by-products "added" to higher-level activity. Don't miss Christ's point: If you seek the higher, the lower will be added in the seeking. Paganism says, "I must have my lower-level needs satisfied *first* if you expect me to seek higher ends." Christ replies, "No, it will not be that way with my disciples. They must put me and other members of my kingdom *first*. All other matters are secondary."

Don't miss the fact that setting lower-level priorities above higher ones is characterized by Christ as adopting a *pagan* philosophy of life. Therefore, unless you wish to place yourself in direct opposition to Jesus Christ in order to stand with pagans, you must reject the Adler/Maslow need theory that undergirds the new self-worth movement. But to do so is to topple the entire edifice.

It is amazing how intelligent Christians can become so enamored with a theory that they must impose it on the Scriptures in such a way that the two are forcibly "integrated" (made to fit by bending the Bible to fit the theory). To demonstrate what I am talking about, let me take you to the pages of an evangelical psychologist who, when propounding self-love doctrine was (quite rightly) asked by a client, "Aren't we to seek *first* the kingdom of God?" He replied:

> Putting a priority on self-acceptance is the
> first step many of us need to take if we are
> going to build a more positive attitude toward
> ourselves.[4]

His self-esteem views are so strong that he is forced
to override Jesus' plain words of priority! Pagan
thought wins out. In her insistence that the counselor
take Matthew 6:33 seriously, the client showed herself
more perceptive and more biblical than her counselor.
We cannot fail to notice that whereas the writer places
his emphasis on self, in Matthew 6 Jesus bids us look
away from our selves, our "needs," our worries, and
our cares. He points us instead to *His* kingdom and *His*
righteousness; He wants us to focus our concern on
Himself and on the other members of His kingdom.
Plainly, Jesus' priorities differ from those in modern
self-worth need theory. You can't follow the pagan
priorities so clearly described by Jesus and at the same
time the priorities that He advocated. You will follow
one or the other, but not both, for they are antithetical.
You can no more follow both than you can go east and
west at the same time.

Bonaro Overstreet vividly describes the cruel fate
of those who live according to the principles of this
pagan, self-seeking worldview. Speaking of the in-
satiable desire that this worldly way of life fosters in
the one who follows it, he writes:

> The problem of his own worth, and of his
> status among his human fellows, remains for
> him, accordingly, one he can neither resolve
> nor leave alone. It nags at him until it blocks

every avenue by which he might make a free,
creative, affectionate approach to life.[5]

In other words, he becomes more and more wrapped
up in himself. Rather than freeing him for higher-level
activity, his pagan priorities make him a slave to himself and his own self-interests. Overstreet speaks of
those who develop "a consuming desire *to take in*
from their world—to take in love, comfort, approval,
protection, reassurance, adulation"[6] rather than to give
out. This list sounds much like the need list indicated
in the "hierarchy of needs." Of course, Overstreet's
solutions to the problem are as wide of the mark as
those which created it in the first place because he does
not approach the difficulty from a biblical perspective.
Pagan thought emphasizes getting what you need
(or, rather, what you *think* you need) while godly
thought emphasizes giving God the honor and service
in His church that He deserves totally apart from
whether your needs are met or not. Using the need
theory, there would be no Christian martyrs. Mission-
aries like Paul would be unavailable. Christ would not
have died. Those who accept the philosophy of self-
esteem as their theoretical worldview—and the New
Reformation is offering nothing less than a total
worldview—seem all too ready to follow its precepts
in real life. If my "needs" must be served at all costs
first, before I am able to serve others, how could I be
expected to give up my life, my goods, or my welfare
for the Lord or for another believer? After all, that is
asking the very highest-level, most self-actualized
activity of me!
The self-esteem need theory—the emphasis on

having my own needs met first—puts a person in the same camp as pagans: "For all these things the Gentiles eagerly seek" (Matthew 6:32). And that is exactly what this "New Reformation" is doing to the Christian church: bringing us back to the humanism from which Christ rescued us! If for no other reason, any movement that rests on such flimsy, flawed underpinnings and that advocates a world-view characterized by Jesus Himself as "pagan" must be rejected.

It is time to close this chapter even though I still must say more about "need." First, however, read the following words from Scripture:

> For this reason I say to you, Do not be anxious for your life, as to what you shall eat, or what you shall drink; nor for your body, as to what you shall put on. Is not life more than food, and the body than clothing? Look at the birds of the air, that they do not sow, neither do they reap, nor gather into barns, and yet your heavenly Father feeds them. Are you not worth much more than they? And which of you by being anxious can add a single cubit to his life's span? And why are you anxious about clothing? Observe how the lilies of the field grow; they do not toil nor do they spin, yet I say to you that even Solomon in all his glory did not clothe himself like one of these. But if God so arrays the grass of the field, which is alive today and tomorrow is thrown into the furnace, will He not much more do so for you, O men of little faith? Do not be anxious then, saying, "What shall we eat?"

or "What shall we drink?" or "With what shall we clothe ourselves?" For all these things the Gentiles eagerly seek; for your heavenly Father knows that you need all these things. But seek first His kingdom and His righteousness and all these things shall be added to you. Therefore do not be anxious for tomorrow, for tomorrow will care for itself. Each day has enough trouble of its own.[7]

Think carefully about what you have learned concerning self-image teaching. If necessary, go back and skim the previous chapters in this book, listening once more to what self-esteem writers are teaching. Compare and contrast their words with what the Lord has to say. Such a comparison leads to one, and only one conclusion: The New Reformation is wrong!

5

More About "Need"

So far we have seen that the Adler/Maslow need theory on which the self-esteem system is built is pagan. It opposes the way of life that Jesus set forth in Matthew 6 and leads unwary Christians away from the abundant life that could be theirs. We have seen that for the Christian the choice lies between a humanistic worldview that puts man first and a biblical view that puts God and His concerns first. This alone should be enough to cause us to steer clear of such teaching. However, there is a great deal more to be said about the dangers of this movement.

In an earlier chapter I called your attention to an important implication of self-worth philosophy: If a person cannot love God or his neighbor (and such love is precisely what is involved in seeking God's kingdom and His righteousness) until his own self-esteem "needs" are first met, this means that a Christian deprived of such lower-level need satisfaction must not

be held responsible for failure to love other people
because, until his image of himself is raised to a satis-
fying level, he will remain *incapable* of such love.

Those who build the foundations of their view of
the human spirit on the principles of self-worth would
cry that Wesner Fallaw is all wrong when he says, "The
surest way to personal worthlessness and personality
destruction lies. through habitual turning within the
self."[1] "No, Mr. Fallaw," say the self-esteemer proponents, "you have it all backward. It is a sense of worthlessness and personal destruction that incapacitates.
And it is only by turning within to remedy the condition, and focusing the whole of our counseling attention on the problem that the counselee has with
himself, that we will ever be able to help such a
Christian to escape the inner devastation brought about
by other people who over the years have deprived
and denigrated him. Instead, we must arrive on the
scene as soon as possible and belatedly administer all
the missing strokes before it is too late to help the
counselee to build a better self-image. At length, if the
destruction is not too serious, he may be able, at least
in part, to fulfil his obligations toward God and other
people."

As we search the Scriptures, we find no such teaching. Everywhere Christians are held responsible for loving God and their neighbors. No excuses are accepted,
no extenuating circumstances allowed. If the apostles
were aware of this all-important matter of bolstering
self-esteem (as they would have been, since they
were inspired by the Holy Spirit in their writing of
the Scriptures), surely they would have said something about it. Yet nowhere do we find them telling

converted pagans in Corinth, in Thessalonica, in Crete, or anywhere else that God does not expect them to love Him or one another until they develop better self-images. This is extraordinarily strange, since these raw pagan converts did not all grow up in exemplary homes and communities. Could it be that none of them suffered the deprivation of proper strokes?

If anything, their backgrounds must have been filled with self-seeking, since they were inclined to "think too highly of themselves" and had to be warned against holding "puffed up" ideas of their own worth: "Through the grace given to me I say to every man among you not to think more highly of himself than he ought to think, but to think so as to have sound judgment, as God has allotted to each a measure of faith" (Romans 12:3); "Knowledge makes arrogant, but love edifies" (1 Corinthians 8:1). The New Testament evidence is exactly opposite to that which the self-worth proponents should expect to find!

Of course, it would be possible for Christians who hold self-esteem doctrines to say that the insights of this movement were not uncovered until the twentieth century. But that would impale them on one or the other horns of a dilemma: 1) For centuries God withheld from His church truth that is essential to fruitful Christian living, or 2) God doesn't think that self-image teaching is all that essential after all. Bible-believing Christians cannot admit to the first of these opinions, since God has said in the Bible that He has given us "*all things* necessary for life and godliness." Nor can they admit to the second possibility so long as they hold to self-esteem dogmas, since those doctrines commit them to the proposition that a good self-image is absolutely essential for fruitful Christian living.

What do the writers of the New Testament epistles actually require of their readers? Quite the opposite of self-image practices. They constantly insist that their readers love God and one another in spite of any deprivation they may have experienced in their backgrounds. Indeed, the issue of deprivation is never raised as an extenuating circumstance to explain away sinful living. Are we to infer that the recipients of the epistles had none of the deprivations of which Maslow and others make so much? Surely not. If self-esteem dogma is to be followed, wouldn't you expect the New Testament writers to say a great deal about how we must stroke these new converts? Wouldn't you expect to see stroke after stroke given to converts in the epistles rather than commands and exhortations to love God and love one another? Commands to love, regardless of background and even in the midst of existing problems of every kind, appear in 1 Corinthians 13 and innumerable other passages. Indeed, Jesus Himself told us that Scripture can be summed up as a group of books that teach us how to love God and one another. If that is so, how is it that the all-important self-worth truth (that love for others rests on love for self, and this in turn on the love of others for one's self) is not spelled out in Scripture?

We must now turn to another question related to need. What kind of situation will we have on our hands if we adopt self-worth views and teach them in our pulpits, in our schools, and in our homes? There will be myriads of sad saints like Midge, wallowing in self-pity because they have been told that, since they have been deprived, they *can't* obey God. To the extent that

MORE ABOUT "NEED" 55

they follow the advice of self-esteem leaders, we will meet Christians who are not only miserable, but miserable to be with: "A person whose interests constantly turn within himself is unlovely and soon unwanted."[2] Moreover, "He may become ineffectual as he suffers excessive concern about his social, occupational, and physical well-being."[3]

With all the supposed concern about the dignity of man that self-esteem proponents regularly express, one would think they would have developed principles and practices that truly dignify man. Is man dignified when he is told that he has become less than a responsible being if he failed to receive sufficient strokes as an infant? To picture me as a helpless pawn in the hands of others who can do or undo me at will fails to convince me that I am all that worthy a being. Is not a person who is judged guilty before God for not measuring up to His standards when he might have, and knows it, who is in the predicament in which he finds himself because of his own sin and who knows that he can change through repentance and sanctification if he only will, a far more dignified person?

One Christian writer says, "We have substituted desire for need and need for desire."[4] He is absolutely correct. In self-esteem writings where the word "need" appears it is frequently possible, and more accurate, to substitute the word "desire." As a matter of fact, several years ago I wrote a few paragraphs on this subject which seem apropos to quote in this context:

"Need!" What a greatly abused term in counseling! Over the last couple of years, again and again the word comes leaping from the page in a jarring way. I am not speaking only of how non-Christian writers misuse it; no, I am especially perturbed at the way believers do. Consider the following:

> The behavior comes not of the Spirit, but of the flesh. It "feels right" because the person is fulfilling the needs of a maladaptive personality.

> . . . The narcissist doesn't really believe this himself; this is why he needs many people to assure him repeatedly.

> The need to be right and the tendency toward self-justification are marks of the exploiter. It is easy for him to confuse good leadership with his need to be right and to win.[5]

Obviously, from these quotations, Bustanoby knows that what he is talking about is sin. He calls the behavior in question "of the flesh," etc. Then why call *sinful* behavior a "need"? Who needs it?

Do you see what I mean? No? Then let me give you another example or two (and I haven't searched for these quotations; they are taken from books lying on my desk at the moment), this time from non-Christian sources:

> Each person in a marriage must satisfy the basic need called stimulus hunger.[6]

All the rest come from various non-Christians who

are discussing adultery, why they took up swinging (wife/husband swapping), and what they got out of it:

> . . . now I seem to have the need for another lover as well.

> Well, it has to do with our own ego needs.

> This conversation is interesting because we're talking about our needs and trying to identify the tensions and the interplay of our needs.

> So you just sort of construct a world that suits your needs.[7]

Now, do you begin to see what I am talking about? The supposed needs (need to be right, need for someone to assure him, stimulus hunger, sex with someone else's spouse) are not *needs* at all.

According to the Scriptures, one's *needs* are relatively few: "If we have food and covering, with these we shall be content" (1 Timothy 6:8). And even these two needs are not to be a source of concern or worry: "For all these things the Gentiles eagerly seek; your heavenly Father knows that you need all these things."

What, then, are these so-called "needs"? Substitute the word *desire* for *need* wherever it occurs [in these quotations] and you will have a biblical picture of what we have been talking about.

Why make so much of the terminology? Because of this important fact: Under the guise of meeting needs, sin is excused. (Some Christian psychologists don't intend to excuse such behavior, but they use terminology that does so in a most confusing manner.) These

are not only desires, but *sinful desires,* and that is why
I am stressing the importance of using correct terminology in counseling. Much harm has been done in this
field by those who under the cover of inexact terms
have justified or (perhaps unwittingly) given counselees
an excuse to justify almost every error and sin that a
person could imagine.

Biblical counselors must be careful when using the
word *need*[8] to refer to what the Bible calls a need, and
nothing else. Especially, following the example of the
apostle Peter, they must properly identify sinful desire
for what it really is (cf. 1 Peter 1:14; 2:11; 4:2,3;
2 Peter 2:10,18; 3:3).[9]

As a last point on the discussion of need versus
desire, consider this: If you've been reading in the self-
esteem literature at all, you have noticed that strange
new construction of words "I had [have] a need
to . . ." Watch out for whatever follows that kind of
beginning. It is not uncommon for the next words to
be the expression of a desire, possibly even a sinful
one, that is being excused by the opening formula. The
construction, in one form or another, appears all over
self-esteem writings. People used to say "I need . . ."
but now we read "I have a need to . . ." The former
referred to an objective secondary need: "I need a
shovel." The latter refers to a supposed inherent and
subjective need: "I have a need to say it." In your mind
(or, if you care to, in the writing itself) scratch out the
word "need" and substitute the word "desire," and
the result will be a much more accurate reading of the
facts. Nearly always that substitution will enhance your
understanding of the problem.

Now let's consider another important matter. What happens if we leave the realm of theory and measure Stephen or John or Paul or Jesus against Maslow's criteria? On the basis of his hierarchy, it would seem clear that each of these persons was "self-actualized." But now consider Paul's statements:

> We are afflicted in every way, but not crushed; perplexed, but not despairing; persecuted, but not forsaken; struck down, but not destroyed; always carrying about in the body the dying of Jesus, that the life of Jesus also may be manifested in our body (2 Corinthians 4:8-10).

> In everything commending ourselves as servants of God, in much endurance, in afflictions, in hardships, in distresses, in beatings, in imprisonments, in tumults, in labors, in sleeplessness, in hunger, in purity, in knowledge, in patience, in kindness, in the Holy Spirit, in genuine love, in the word of truth, in the power of God (2 Corinthians 6:4-7).

> Are they servants of Christ? (I speak as if insane) I more so; in far more labors, in far more imprisonments, beaten times without number, often in danger of death. Five times I received from the Jews thirty-nine lashes. Three times I was beaten with rods, once I was stoned, three times I was shipwrecked, a night and a day I have spent in the deep. I

have been on frequent journeys, in dangers from rivers, dangers from robbers, dangers from my countrymen, dangers from the Gentiles, dangers in the city, dangers in the wilderness, dangers on the sea, dangers among false brethren; I have been in labor and hardship, through many sleepless nights, in hunger and thirst, often without food, in cold and exposure. Apart from such external things, there is the daily pressure upon me of concern for all the churches (2 Corinthians 11:23-28).

According to the record it would seem that Paul had few strokes—mainly strikes! How was it that a person so "deprived" could spend his entire adult life in loving service for Christ and other people? Surely there is something wrong with the basic self-love thesis when it so poorly fits the great apostle. Why didn't he suffer from a crippling self-image and from debilitating low self-esteem if it is possible for other people to produce this in a human being by their failure to treat him properly?

Just compare some of the incidents in the life of Paul mentioned in the above-quoted verses from 2 Corinthians with Maslow's hierarchy of needs and you'll find that they simply don't compute. After that, try comparing Isaiah 53 with levels 1 and 4 in Maslow's pyramid:

(1) In order to be well-adjusted, you must reach the stage of self-actualization.

and

(2) In order to reach that stage you must pass through the other four stages first; your physical and personal needs must be met before you are in a position to become self-actualized.[10]

Tell this to Paul, or to Stephen, or . . . to Christ!

6

Love...As Yourself?

"But," you ask, "how could Christians so blindly accept self-esteem dogma? What we have seen so far seems devastating to the theory. And, on top of that, there isn't a scrap of biblical evidence to support it."

Yes, you're exactly right. But Christians who propagate these teachings do make a feeble show at finding self-esteem principles and practices in the Bible. While admitting that it was the unbelieving psychologists from whom they took their lead, they have made every attempt possible to scrape up some biblical support. The Scriptures are ransacked and verses are twisted in order to give some sort of biblical credence to the theory. But the Bible is used not to *discover* what God has to say or what to believe; rather, the viewpoint was already bought and brought to the Bible when the biblical search began.

That methodology is always dangerous. Yet it has

been the stock-in-trade of Christians who are psychologists: A pagan system is adopted; then the Bible is said to support it. First it was Freud's view of the "id" that was supposed to approximate the Bible's teaching on original sin. Then, since Jung made religious statements now and then, he was said to be "close" to Christianity. (Of course, that his thinking confessedly is based on such "religious" views as those found in the Tibetan *Book of the Dead* was rarely mentioned.) Next, Carl Rogers' views on listening and acceptance were readily likened to biblical ideas (even though statements in Proverbs 18 and elsewhere oppose Rogerian thought and practice in both areas). Then Skinner's behaviorism was equated with scriptural statements about reward and punishment (without taking notice of the fact that the latter are conditioned by God's eternal reward-and-punishment program, and thereby are entirely different). Now, as the latest fad, it is self-worth dogma that is said to be similar or identical to biblical doctrine.

This penchant for "finding" the latest psychological ideas in the Scriptures is dangerous for several reasons:

1. The extrabiblical view is given biblical authority in the eyes of many Christians. To answer the question with which this chapter began, the reason that so many Christians are led into the acceptance of psychological views is that these views are given a biblical cast and are supported by biblical passages that have been wrenched out of place and made to do service that they were never intended to do. Unfortunately,

many Christians are deceived into thinking that the Bible really does teach such things.

2. God is misrepresented. This, of course, is the most dangerous fact of all. That Christian psychologists (very few of whom take the time to become competent in serious exegesis) can use the Word of the living God in such a cavalier fashion as they sometimes do, and that undiscerning Christians so readily accept their interpretations, is both frightening and appalling. Passages are distorted and misused with abandon; the Scriptures are made to say what the interpreter wants them to say; and the Bible, as if it were made of wax, is shaped to fit the latest fad. There is a certain lack of reverence for God Himself evidenced in this process.

3. Any system that proposes to solve human problems apart from the Bible and the power of the Holy Spirit (as all of these pagan systems, including the self-worth system, do) is automatically condemned by Scripture itself. Neither Adler nor Maslow professed Christian faith. Nor does their system in any way depend upon the message of salvation. Love, joy, peace, etc., are discussed as if they were not the fruit of the Spirit but merely the fruit of right views of one's self which anyone can attain without the Bible or the work of the Spirit in his heart.

For these reasons the self-worth system with its claimed biblical correspondences must be rejected. It does not come from the Bible; Christians called the Bible into service long after the system was developed by others who had no intention of basing their system on God's Word. Any resemblance between biblical teaching and the teaching of the self-worth originators is either contrived or coincidental.

But, because Christians have attempted to make a biblical case for this unbiblical substitute for God's way of helping men, we must take a hard look at the principal passages that have been forced into service. There are three: 1) Matthew 22:36-40, 2) Romans 6/Colossians 3, and 3) James 3:9.

> "Teacher, which is the great commandment in the Law?" And He said to him, "You shall love the Lord your God with all your heart, and with all your soul, and with all your mind. This is the great and foremost commandment. The second is like it: You shall love your neighbor as yourself. On these two commandments depend the whole Law and the Prophets" (Matthew 22:36-40).

Together with these verses, we shall also have occasion to look at the parallel passage in Luke 10:25-37.

For purposes of our discussion, the most important verse is Matthew 22:39b: "You shall love your neighbor as yourself." This is probably the verse most quoted by advocates of self-worth, self-esteem teaching. Trobisch, for instance, calls it a "command to love yourself,"[1] and says:

> Self-love is thus the prerequisite and the criterion for our conduct towards our neighbor.[2]

That is an astonishing statement! Trobisch is telling us not only that Jesus commanded us to love ourselves, but that we cannot love our neighbor properly unless we first learn to love ourselves because the criterion, or standard, by which we determine how to love a neighbor is how we love ourselves!

He has the temerity to say, "This [the finding of modern psychology that man must acquire a love for himself] sheds new light on the command which Jesus emphasized as ranking in importance next to loving God." In other words, Trobisch thinks that until modern psychologists unearthed the truth elsewhere, this important biblical command—in this very important new aspect—lay buried and was not adequately understood! For nearly 2000 years the church was in the dark!

In truth, the verse says nothing of the sort. Consider the facts. First, there is no command here (or anywhere else in the Bible) to love yourself. Does that surprise you? To hear self-image leaders talk, you would think the Bible contained little else. But in fact there is no command here or elsewhere in Scripture to love yourself.

Christ made it perfectly clear that He was talking about two, and only two, commandments. In verses 39 and 40 He speaks of the "*second*" commandment and "these *two* commandments." There is no third commandment. All of Scripture can be hung on two pegs: Love God, love neighbor. Yet the self-esteem people make three commandments out of Christ's two! There is absolutely no excuse for treating the Scriptures in this manner.

As if such distortion of plain scriptural teaching were not enough, they go further and make the first two commandments depend upon the supposed "third."

According to the Adler/Maslow hierarchy, lower-level needs must be satisfied before higher-level needs can be. This means that level 4 (self-esteem) needs must be met before level 5 (self-actualizing) needs can be. Or, to put it in terms of the verse that is being forced into the Adler/Maslow system, you cannot love your neighbor (a level 5 activity) until you first learn to love yourself (a level 4 activity). That is why Trobisch maintains "Self-love is thus the prerequisite" for loving your neighbor. He goes on to say:

> You cannot love your neighbor, you cannot love God unless you first love yourself. . . . Without self-love there can be no love for others.[3]

This way of thinking is not confined to Walter Trobisch. Remember Crabb's statement of the case:

> In order to be well-adjusted, you must reach the stage of self-actualization. In order to reach that stage you must pass through the other four stages first. . . .[4]

Now listen to Philip Captain:

> Actually our ability to love God and to love our neighbor is limited by our ability to love ourselves. We cannot love God more than we love our neighbor and we cannot love our neighbor more than we love ourselves.[5]

Captain has even refined the hierarchy with a twist of his own: Love for God is dependent on love for neighbor, which in turn is dependent on love for self.

In each of these constructions the writer is thoroughly convinced that love for God and neighbor is contingent on love for one's self. But in the biblical passage not only is there no third commandment, but neither is any dependent relationship set up between the two commandments. Both of these self-esteem claims are brought to the text to reshape it; then, in its reshaped form, the text is forced into the system.

Jesus actually *presupposes* a love of self in this passage. He says, "You must love your neighbor as yourself." The command is to love your neighbor *as you already love yourself.* The verse could be translated literally, "You must love your neighbor as you are loving yourself."

The same self-love that is presupposed by Jesus is likewise presupposed in Paul's argument in Ephesians 5:28,29, where he urges husbands to love their wives "as you love [are loving] your own body." He goes on to say:

> No one ever hated his own flesh, but nourishes and cherishes it, just as Christ also does the church.

In other words, Paul's entire argument turns on the fact that we already exhibit love for ourselves.

Comparing Luke 10:29 with Matthew 22:36-40, an important contextual addition appears. Luke tells us, "Wishing to justify himself, he [the lawyer whose words occasioned the discussion] said to Jesus, 'And who is my neighbor?' " Whereupon Jesus told the parable of the Good Samaritan.

What was the lawyer's problem? Was he suffering from a loss of self-esteem? Quite the contrary. Luke says that "he wanted to *justify* himself." That is to say, the question he raised, "Who is my neighbor?" was not really asked for information but to stump Jesus. And notice that he wanted to stump Him *so that he could justify his own sinful ways.* It was asked, therefore, out of *self*-interest. He liked himself the way he was and did not want to give of his time or money to his neighbor. He wished to remain all wrapped up in himself.

The parable of the Good Samaritan certainly was not designed to foster a higher *self*-interest, but just the opposite. The very point of the parable is that one must love his neighbor—i.e. anyone in need—as himself. He must look after the needs of others and even put himself out for others. Jesus did not say that in order to engage in such high-level activity as the Samaritan did one must first come to a place where all his own needs at lower levels were satisfied. What of the priest and the Levite? Were they deprived? Did they have low self-esteem? Of course not. They probably considered themselves far better than the Samaritan. Their problem was the same as the lawyer's: They loved themselves so much that they would not put themselves out for anyone else.

Trobisch tells us that our love for ourselves is the "criterion" as well as the prerequisite for loving others. He explains this by saying, "It is the measuring stick for loving others which Jesus gives us."[6] What he is claiming is that when Jesus said "Love your neighbor as yourself" He meant "*Do the same things for others* that you do for yourself." But that couldn't be right for several reasons. First, the criteria for loving others are the Ten Commandments that Jesus was here summarizing in two: "You shall love the Lord your God with all your heart, and with all your soul, and with all your strength, and with all your mind; and your neighbor as yourself" (Luke 10:27). By saying that all the books of the Bible (the law and the prophets) could be summed up in those two commandments, He was also pointing to the Scriptures as the outworking of the commandments in everyday life. In effect, then, Jesus was saying that the criteria for loving God and others are to be found in the Bible—not in us.

Clearly we must love our neighbors as the Bible commands, and not by doing the same things for them that we do for ourselves. Out of self-love we do not only good things, but all sorts of injurious and sinful things to ourselves: We commit adultery, we lie, we steal, we eat too much, we commit suicide, etc. Things we do for ourselves, then, are not the criteria for loving others.

What then do Jesus' words "as yourself" mean? There is no thought of criteria in them, since, plainly, the criteria were to be found in the Ten Commandments and their outworking in all of Scripture. The thought has to do with *intensity, fervency,* and *amount of love.* Notice carefully that Jesus says the second commandment is just like the first (Matthew 22:39). In what respects are the two alike? First, they both speak of love; they are both commands to love. But that cannot be the primary likeness to which Jesus was pointing; it is too obvious to make a point of. There is a second way in which the two commandments are alike. Jesus' command to love God "with

all your heart, and with all your soul, and with all your
mind" (v. 37) means with all you are and all you have.
It means to love God genuinely and sincerely, fervently
and wholeheartedly. It is in this respect that the two
commandments are "just alike." When you are commanded to love your neighbor "as yourself," it means
to love him just as wholeheartedly as you love yourself!

We already have a *fervent, dedicated, genuine,* and
sincere love for ourselves. With sinners, this love is
almost always excessive. Now, says Jesus, extend the
same amount of love toward your neighbor: Love him
"as yourself." The argument is precisely the same as
the argument that Paul makes for a husband loving his
wife "just as" he *already* loves his own body. How
is that to be done? In the same fervent, nourishing, and
cherishing attitude with which a man cares for himself (not necessarily by *doing* the same things to his
wife that he does to himself).

It is plain that Matthew 22, supposedly the strongest
passage supporting self-worth, is actually aimed directly at the movement itself. Any serious consideration of this passage completely repudiates the kind of
self-love teaching we see today.

To sum up this chapter, we must love our neighbors
as ourselves. But Matthew 22:39 contains no commandment to love one's self, since we need not be
concerned about learning to love ourselves if we truly
love God and our neighbors. Since the fulfillment of
these two commandments is the fulfillment of all, we
will always do the right things for ourselves. Love, in
the Bible, is a matter of *giving*: "God so loved the
world that He *gave*..." (John 3:16); "He loved me
and *gave*..." (Galatians 2:20 KJV); "Husbands, love

your wives, just as Christ also loved the church and *gave* Himself..." (Ephesians 5:25). Because it is more blessed to give than to receive, the self-love proponents (who advocate getting from others and *giving to self* before giving to God and others) take away a rich blessing from those who follow their unbiblical emphasis. There is no need for concern about how to love one's self, for so long as one seeks first to love God and his neighbor in a biblical fashion, all proper self-concern will appear as a by-product. That is why the Bible never commands us to love ourselves. Since the Bible is silent on the matter, we should be too.

7

Of Infinite Worth?

Now it is time to look at Romans 6/Colossians 3 and James 3:9.

First we must think about the sections from Paul's two letters. In the parallel passages found in Romans 6 and Colossians 3 the believer is told to "consider" himself dead to sin and alive to God. He is assured that he is a new person in God's sight and that the old person he used to be is legally dead. In addition, he is exhorted to become, in everyday living, the new person that he is counted to be in God's sight in Christ.

Self-image theorists have been quick to pounce on these passages, turning them to their own purposes and giving little or no consideration to the purposes for which they were written. It is clear from even a cursory reading of the two chapters that Paul had no intention whatever of teaching self-worth doctrine. And no Christians ever found such teaching in these passages over a 1900-year period until humanistic psychologists "alerted" them to the dogmas that they now profess to find so plainly taught there. Nevertheless, self-esteem advocates take comfort in what they think they can make these passages say.

One zealous advocate of the system claims:

> Our self-image as Christians, therefore, must be of ourselves as persons who have decisively rejected the old way of living which is called the old man, and have permanently adopted the new way of living which is called the new man.

In support of this he cites Romans 6:11: "Even consider yourselves to be dead to sin, but alive to God in Christ Jesus." Then, to make his point, he insists that—

> This is as clear a biblical statement of the Christian's self-image as one can find anywhere.[1]

If the professor who made that statement is correct, and if no clearer "biblical statement" of the doctrine is to be found, then the movement is in grave trouble. The fact is that there is nothing clear about self-image in the passage at all.

True, Colossians 3 and Romans 6 tells us that as God looks at us "in Christ" our standing before Him as Judge is perfect; no fault can be found. We have been completely forgiven when we believed, and now God sees us as brand-new people in His Son. *In Him* all the old ways have gone and the new ways have come to stay. All that is wonderfully clear. But what is also clear is that Paul does not tell us this to "make us feel good about ourselves" or to "give us strokes" or to "raise our self-esteem." His purpose is *to urge us to become in everyday living what we already are counted to be in Christ.* In other words, he wants us to see that *in ourselves* we fall far short of what we are *in Christ*.

Listen to Romans 6:1,2:

> What shall we say then? Are we to continue in sin that grace might increase? May it never be! How shall we who died to sin still live in it?

Verse 2 sounds more like an exhortation than a stroke! The professor who quoted Romans 6:11 was selective; to give the full sense, he should have quoted the next verses also. Verses 12 and 13 continue Paul's thought: "Therefore do not let sin reign in your mortal body that you should obey its lusts, and do not go on presenting the members of your body to sin. . . ." What is clear is that Paul's purpose in urging us to "consider" ourselves dead to sin and alive to righteousness in Christ is to get us to live differently. The "therefore" with which verse 12 begins introduces the conclusion that we should draw from the fact stated in verse 11. Paul does *not* say, "Therefore you ought to feel good about yourselves." He *does* say, "In daily life start living up to the high standard of your legal standing in Christ."

Paul, writing to the Colossians, states:

> For you have died and your life is hidden with Christ in God. . . . Therefore consider the

> members of your earthly body as dead to
> immorality, impurity, passion, evil desire, and
> greed, which amounts to idolatry. . . . But
> now you also, put them all aside: anger,
> wrath, malice, slander, and abusive speech
> from your mouth. Do not lie to one another,
> since you laid aside the old self with its evil
> practices, and have put on the new self who
> is being renewed to a true knowledge accord-
> ing to the image of the One who created him
> (Colossians 3:3,5,8-10).

Again, the fact that the old life has been replaced by
the new life in Christ is affirmed. And again, just as
surely as before, what Paul makes of it is this: Since
this is true in Christ, in your everyday affairs start living
like it is true. There isn't the slightest whisper in these
passages about looking on ourselves as people of great
worth or about gaining a better self-image. All he is
doing is holding up the ideal (our perfect standing in
Christ) and urging us to approximate it more fully in
ourselves.

Do these passages warrant us to say anything like
the following Christian writer does?

> . . . we must view ourselves as uniquely won-
> derful, intrinsically valuable.[2]

Certainly not! The purpose of these passages is to
show us the great gap between what we are *counted
or reckoned to be in Christ* (justification) and what we
actually are in ourselves in daily living (sanctification), *in order to urge us to close the gap.* They are

designed not to make us satisfied with ourselves so that we may accept ourselves as we are, but to *destroy* any self-satisfaction that may exist and to motivate us to make greater progress in Christian living. Nothing could be better designed to thoroughly reduce any sense of pride, worth, or satisfaction to which we may cling than to hold up before us our perfection in Christ and then ask us to compare our actual performance with it! Romans 6 and Colossians 3 effectively attack self-esteem teaching rather than bolster it.

These passages, then, were not written to make us feel better about ourselves but to show us how God sees us in Jesus so as to spur us on to more consistent Christian living. There is great potential in the new life that we have in Christ, but we will never begin to realize it if we sit around thinking about how worthy we are.

Now we come to James 3:9 and its Old Testament background found in Genesis 1:27 and 9:6:

> With it [the tongue] we bless our Lord and Father; and with it we curse men, who have been made in the likeness of God (James 3:9).

> God created man in His own image, in the image of God He created him; male and female He created them. . . . Whoever sheds man's blood, by man his blood shall be shed, for in the image of God He made man (Genesis 1:27; 9:6).

The operative words in these verses are "image" and "likeness." Self-image thinkers are quick to point out

(correctly) that in these passages man is said to be in
God's image not only before the fall but afterward.
Since in Ephesians 4:24 and in Colossians 3:10 we are
told that God's image and likeness are being *renewed*
in the believer, it is certain that the full image and
likeness did not remain after the fall; nevertheless
something that the writers of Genesis 9 and James 3
could still call God's "image" and "likeness" did
remain. It is not important to discuss distinctions between what might be called man's moral and intellectual likeness and his constitutional likeness at this
point, since they contribute nothing to the question
under consideration. What is certain is that, in some
sense, man is still in God's likeness.

Further, let us observe that penalties and warning
as well as rebukes and exhortations are adduced from
the fact that man is God's image-bearer. Those who
curse other people or take their lives do so at great peril
just because of that fact. Self-esteem proponents have
interpreted these biblical sanctions in an unacceptable
manner.

Listen to some of the self-worth arguments:

> Does this [the fall of man] mean that man now
> became a being of no worth? Nothing could be
> further from the truth. Even after the fall man
> was still considered to be a being of infinite
> worth . . . The Scriptures . . . affirm that even
> fallen man still bears the image of God.[3]

Another writes:

> Even New Testament writers recognize the

image of God in man. James warns against cursing because they are made in the likeness of God.

He believes that this—

is the bedrock for self-esteem. We are created by the hand of God and in His image.[4]

A third rhapsodizes about—

the nobility, uniqueness, meaning, worth and significance of man.

All of these, he assures us—

rest on his being made in the image of God.[5]

It is true that man is still in God's image in some sense (though the moral and intellectual image has been so defaced that it must be restored), but what does this mean? The fact itself says nothing at all about self-esteem or self-worth. In none of the contexts in which the image of God in man is mentioned does the writer use that fact to teach the kinds of things that we have been reading in the quotations above. How is it possible to extrapolate the idea that man is "of infinite worth" from the fact that he was created in God's image? The one concept does not follow logically from the other. Moreover, man's nature, which bears God's image, is never held out as a reason for having high self-esteem.

Then why are we warned so sharply against assaulting God by assaulting man, God's image-bearer? Here is the crux of the matter, and it is here that the self-esteem writers go astray.

Consider this: I show you a photograph of my wife. If you curse it, make fun of it, spit on it, and tear it up—you will have to answer to me!

"Why?" you ask. "After all, it's only a *photograph*."

Yes, but it is a photograph of *my wife*! That is what makes all the difference.

The picture itself—the paper and ink, etc.—is not of much value. It is worth only a few cents. What is of concern to me is not the picture itself but the one whom it represents.

Intrinsically man is worth little; he is certainly not of "infinite worth." No created finite being, whether fallen or unfallen, unredeemed or redeemed, could be. The warnings of Genesis 9 and James 3 do not stem from the fact of man's infinite worth; rather, they stem from the fact of *God's* infinite worth! To dishonor man and to abuse him is to dishonor and abuse God because he is made in God's image. That is what brings the warning and the penalty. It is *the One whose image and likeness man bears* that is of significance—not the man who bears that image and likeness. He is merely the photograph.

Recently a seminary student told a criminal in jail who thought he was "nothin' ":

> William, you ain't nothin'. God made you in
> His image. You have infinite worth in His
> eyes.[6]

Why didn't he tell him that he was a sinner who was in desperate condition apart from the saving grace of Christ? That the infinite God took on human flesh and died on a cross to pay the penalty for sinners like him, and that by believing he could now have eternal life?

Since we have encountered such statements as "infinite worth" applied to man in more than one place, let's follow that line of thinking just a bit further. Outlandish claims are made for man, claims that one would expect to hear only from pantheists or humanists who place man on God's throne. Here are just a few:

> . . . the human being is a glorious, dignified creature with infinite value.[7]

> God wants us to *see ourselves as his gift to the world.*[8]

> We are something beautiful that God has done. We are something exquisite that he has planned.[9]

Where is the biblical precedent for using such language? Certainly nothing like it can be found in the entire Bible. Wouldn't you think that any writer, speaking in God's name, would be careful to talk as the Bible does? These writers, and many more like them, seem to have thrown off all restraint in their desire to glorify man.

Here is what a third writer opines:

> By creation, every human being is a unique
> person of great worth and dignity.[10]

I shall let these statements, all made by professed
evangelicals who are deeply involved in propagating
self-worth teaching, speak for themselves. When you
can find anything like what they are saying in the Scriptures you should take them seriously. Until that time
you should write off their words as totally misguided.

Occasionally the self-worth enthusiast will refer to
Matthew 6:26, "Are you not worth much more than they
[the birds]?" or Matthew 10:31, "You are of more value
than many sparrows," or Luke 12:7, "You are of more
value than many sparrows." The enthusiast will then
make the point that "here is a statement about man's
great value!" The passages are used to show man's
"infinite value" to God. But do they?

Examine them closely; notice what Jesus actually
says. Let us ask two questions: 1) How much value is
man said to have? 2) To whom is he said to be of
value?

In the passages Jesus is explicit: Two sparrows are
sold for a cent, and five for two cents. Man is said to
be more valuable than "many sparrows." This means
that if "many" sparrows means 500 sparrows, you are
worth $2.50 at most; if it means 1000 sparrows, your
worth exceeds $5.00! The point is not man's great
worth but God's far-reaching providential care. If it
extends to sparrows, which are worth so little, then
it surely extends to man, who is worth more.

The answer to the second question, To whom is he
said to be of value? grows out of the first. Since Jesus
is discussing value in monetary terms, it is clear that

He is speaking of man's worth (over against a bird's worth) *to other men*. The bird is worth so much to man; a man is worth more. Man's value to God is not in question. The argument from the lesser to the greater on the scale of being has to do with God's providence and *not* with man's value. If, in His infinite goodness, God cares for the birds of the air, won't He care for you, who in the eyes of men are worth more?

If self-image enthusiasts wish to say that God counts man's worth to Him monetarily, and that this worth amounts to something that compares to sparrows, the fact is hardly calculated to bolster one's self-worth! The comparison can only serve to cool enthusiasm, not foster it.

The fact is that these verses teach nothing whatever about self-esteem.

In the following chapter I shall have occasion to show that man is of value only to other men, and not to God at all. Let us turn, then, to a discussion of worth from another perspective.

8

Worthy of Salvation?

Along with the many other problems in the self-worth movement is one that stands out for its close affinity to heresy. I want to make it clear at the outset that not all who espouse self-esteem tenets adhere to this incipient heresy, although a significant number do. For that reason it must be addressed with clarity.

What is this false belief that borders on heresy? The teaching that *God redeemed man because of his great worth*. In an attempt to exalt man, by supposing him to be of infinite worth, God's grace is unwittingly denied. This denial is unintentional, I presume, because those who assert the false doctrine would in other contexts profess to believe that it was not because of anything in us that God sent His Son, but that He did so only out of pure, unmerited favor and unwarranted love.

Listen to a sample of this error:

> Sinful men are valuable to God. If God loves
> sinful men for the redeemable value He sees
> in them, then we ought to love these men too,
> including ourselves.[1]

Do you understand what the writer said? The point
is that God saved man not out of pure grace, totally
apart from anything in man that would commend him
to God, but rather because of some "redeemable
value" He saw in him. That is to say, man was too
valuable to lose, and *that* is why Christ came to die
on the cross!

The actual teaching of the Bible (and that of the
sixteenth-century reformers and all of orthodox Christianity ever since) is that it was not because of anything God saw in man that He redeemed him, but out
of pure mercy and His determination to set His love
on him. God's love was not the response to man's
lovableness!

Man was created not to become someone in his own
right. He was not created to add something to God,
who before and after creation remains the same—
unchanged, perfect, and complete. No, man was
created to glorify God.

"But," you say, "doesn't *that* add something to
God?" No. When the Bible speaks of "glorifying" God,
it does not mean adding glory to His essential Being. It
means making God's infinite glory known before others
(Matthew 5:16). The Hebrew word for glory (*kabod*)
means "weight" and the Greek word (*doxa*) means
"fame." In Christian thinking neither one thought nor
the other prevails. Rather, the two ideas are combined,
as Paul combined them in 2 Corinthians 4:17 when he

spoke of the "weight of glory." To glorify God is to accord Him His true *weight* in every situation so as to spread His *fame*. In order to display His nature before the universe of angels and men (and any other creatures that may be in it), God created the human race and demonstrated His mercy and wrath in it (Romans 9:22,23). Man was created for the benefit of other created beings, who, in seeing God's nature so displayed, could understand both His justice and power and His mercy and grace. No wonder the angels in heaven rejoice whenever a sinner is saved (Luke 15:7,10)! The cross was not merely an act of compassion and mercy directed toward mankind; it was a cosmic event in which God demonstrated who and what He is before all the universe.

No wonder, then, that we should not think of *man* as the motivating cause of redemption. No, man was not so "valuable to God" that He had to save him. On the contrary, the ultimate cause of salvation was solely in God Himself, who, "*in order to* demonstrate His wrath and to make His power known" and "*in order to* make known the riches of His glory" determined to set His love on rebellious sinners upon this planet, saving those who believe and rejecting those who do not.

Israel's problem was thinking that she was of great value to God. To disabuse her of any other such notion, He told her in no uncertain terms that it was not because of anything in her that He chose her to become His holy nation, but, as He put it, "because the Lord loved you" (Deuteronomy 7:6-8). Divine grace begins in God with His love—not in man with his value. To make redemption at any level depend on man's worth rather than on God's mercy is to do despite to grace.

Listen to another writer desperate to find biblical support for the self-esteem position:

> It is as if Christ had said, "You are of such worth to me that I am going to die; even experience hell so that you might be adopted as my brothers and sisters."[2]

This from a minister who has subscribed to the Westminster Confession of Faith! This confession reads in part:

> God . . . has chosen, in Christ, unto everlasting glory, out of His *mere free grace and love*, without any foresight of faith, or good works, or perseverance in either of them, *or any other thing in the creature as conditions or causes moving Him thereunto*: and all to the praise of His glorious grace (Chapter 3:5) [emphasis mine].

How he can square the two views is beyond me!

The Scriptures teach that "while we were helpless," "while we were sinners," and "while we were enemies," Christ died for us (Romans 5:6,8,10). Why did Paul use such language if we were of infinite worth? We were unlovely, unloving, and unlovable. Of what worth is a weak, sinful enemy of God to Him? Yet, in spite of all that there was in us that might repel Him, God out of His great mercy alone determined to set His love on us. This cannot help but turn our eyes away from ourselves and any supposed self-worth and

instead toward God, who is truly worthy of *all* of our
love and praise for redeeming us!

Now hear another writer from the New Reformation school of thought:

> Of course, the greatest demonstration of a
> person's worth to God was shown in giving
> us His Son.[3]

Right?

Wrong! It was the greatest demonstration of God's
mercy, love, and grace!

Notice how the self-image proponents, like the
humanistic psychologists with whom these ideas originated, keep on focusing on man's great ("infinite")
worth rather than God's great (and truly infinite!) love.

Indeed, for some self-esteem proponents grace has
lost its wonder:

> Many Christians' self-esteem is terribly low.
> They somehow have not come to the place
> of seeing how precious they are to God. They
> even wonder how God could love such a
> person as themselves. They're amazed that
> God forgave their sins in the first place.[4]

I am still amazed; aren't you? I am not at all ready
to rip *Amazing Grace* from my hymnbook! This writer
seems to think that because man is so precious, we
should *expect* God to have redeemed him. What
unbelievable toying with heresy in the name of Christianity! When I cease being amazed that Christ died
to save "such a worm as I," I shall start wondering

about my salvation. This sad response to God's marvelous grace seems all too symptomatic of this movement that is bent on glorifying man rather than God.

Just so you will know how widespread is this teaching
among evangelicals who, whether knowingly or not,
align themselves with the Adler/Maslow theories, I shall
put before you a few more astounding statements.
Notice how, in one way or another, each writer (unwittingly, I trust) denies God's grace by making the
motive for redemption *man's value and worth*. Here
are four more typical specimens by additional writers.

The first writes approvingly:

> Someone has said, "God would never have
> given His only begotten Son to die for junk."[5]

Another says:

> The fact that God gave His Son to die for *you*
> proves how eternally valuable you are.[6]

In a slightly different vein:

> Reminding ourselves of the promises, pur-
> poses and ways of God shows how significant
> we are....[7]

Here not only redemption but *all* that God promises
and does for us is said to be a response on His part to
our significance rather than an act of His love, free
mercy, goodness, and grace!

Finally, note this:

> Man's intrinsic worth and significance as the
> image-bearer of God is magnified by the
> lengths to which God went to redeem him.[8]

Not so! The cross magnifies Christ and His marvelous
grace—not us and our supposed worth. Let us cease
from magnifying man; let us once again magnify the
Lord together and bless *His* holy name!

Where does the Bible teach the things you have been
reading? Nowhere. Everywhere it teaches exactly the
opposite. (Consider, for example, Job 25:5,6; Micah
6:8; Matthew 18:12; 23:12; Romans 3:10-18; 1 Corinthians 1:28,29; Galatians 6:14; Ephesians 4:2; Philip-
pians 2:3-11; Colossians 3:12; James 4:6,10.) To say
that Christ died for us because we were "of great
worth," "valuable to God," and "precious" is to
suppose that in some sense we are *needed* by God.
True, men and women are of some value to one
another—but to God? What do we add to Him? Nothing. To be of value is to be valuable *for something*. But
of what value is man to God? In no way does man
benefit God. Before man existed, the Trinity possessed
perfection of fellowship as well as of being—in total
satisfaction. God did not make man or need him to fill
some emptiness in Himself. He continues—as He was—
self-sufficient. Nothing in man was of such redeemable
value to Him that He had to save man. It is true,
certainly, that as with all He created, God was pleased
with the human race He had created. Truly, before
sin, man was "good, very good." But so was *all*
that God made. And, while it is true that man was
made as the highest of His earthly creation and unique,
yet even then he was created a little lower than the

angels. So, on balance, the place of man is high in reference to the rest of earthly creation (we don't know anything about life in the rest of the universe), but even from what we know, man was not made as the epitome of created beings. This fact all the more exalts Jesus in His humiliation. When He came to die, it wasn't for the greatest being in creation, but because he became one of us and died for men who had descended even lower in their sin. The fact that man, in Christ, has been exalted to the highest place in creation says nothing about man's value or worth, but rather focuses on God's great mercy and grace.

J.I. Packer surely is correct when he writes:

> . . . modern Christians . . . spread a thin layer of Bible teaching over the mixture of popular psychology and common sense they offer, but their overall approach clearly reflects the narcissism—the "selfism" or "meism" as it is sometimes called—that is the way of the world in the modern West.[9]

This chapter may seem shorter than some of the others; I did not think it necessary to reason with the reader to any conclusions. Merely pointing out to those who appreciate the marvelous grace of our Lord Jesus Christ that many proponents among the self-worth movement are tampering with the precious doctrine of grace in order to support a non-Christian humanistic theory should prove adequate in itself.

9

Passages Often Overlooked

What follows in this chapter is in no sense definitive or comprehensive, since the verses I shall cite and discuss are but illustrative of the vast number that might be called into service to refute self-esteem claims. I set them forth in order to offer an adequate, though not exhaustive, treatment of the problem.

There are any number of passages that flatly contradict the grandiose assertions about man that are made by self-worth teachers. Usually these teachers conveniently ignore such passages. That is why you should become acquainted with at least a few of these Scriptures.

Hoekema decries the fact that—

> In some of the official formularies used by evangelical Christian churches...believers are urged to "loathe" or to "abhor" themselves. Again the terminology is unfortunate.[1]

Those who believe such a statement would rather have us *love* ourselves. But, while the Scriptures do not tell us to love ourselves, there is a good bit in them about loathing and abhorring one's self. For example, in Ezekiel 36:31 we read:

> Then you will remember your evil ways and your deeds that were not good, and you will loathe yourselves in your own sight for your iniquities and your abominations.

This passage speaks approvingly of God's people "loathing" themselves "in their own sight." Those last four words, "in their own sight," refer to the *self-image* of those who are truly repentant. When His people go astray, God says, He will bring them to a place where they have such a low self-image that they will loathe themselves. This loathing is not "unfortunate," but commendable in God's sight, because it is a part of repentance. Ezekiel's words are a far cry from the statements that we have been reading about "accepting and loving yourself," "as you are," "unconditionally," and so on.

Note especially that the very word "loathe," condemned by the self-worth writer quoted above, turns out to be God's own Word! You can also find Job saying, "I abhor myself and repent in dust and ashes" (Job 42:6 KJV; see also such passages as Ezekiel 6:9c; 20:43). So "abhor" must be an acceptable word in God's sight too. Yet we are told that the choice of those two words found in the formularies is "unfortunate." Did God err? Where do the self-esteem writers think the formularies got those words in the first place?

Such formularies usually stick very closely to biblical thought and expression. Obviously, the wording came from the Bible itself.

Surely those who have been taught to think of man as "a glorious, dignified creature," "God's gift to the world," and "something beautiful and exquisite" would receive a serious jolt if they listened to God's description of man in the Scriptures! God Himself compares unrepentant man to *nauseating putrefaction* (the meaning of the Hebrew word translated "loathe" in Ezekiel 36:31; 20:43; 6:9).

Consider another emphasis found in Scripture that comes at the question from a different angle. First Corinthians 13:1,2 reads as follows:

> If I speak with the tongues of men and angels, but do not have love, I have become a noisy gong or a clanging cymbal. And if I have the gift of prophecy, and know all mysteries and all knowledge; and if I have all faith, so as to remove mountains, but do not have love, *I am nothing.*

Self-esteem proponents, who speak so much of *getting* love and *being* loved so that their fourth-level needs are met, haven't adequately considered what the person who fails to love others is like. Here God calls him a noisy gong and a clanging cymbal. In fact, he calls him "nothing."

This creates an insuperable problem for the self-worth proponent. Think about it for a moment. According to standard self-worth teaching, a person must be

somebody of worth to himself in order to love others.
But God declares that he is "nothing" *unless and until*
he loves others!

When the prisoner named William told the seminary
student that he was "nothin'," presumably he was
closer to God's estimate than was the student who con-
tradicted him and said that he was of "infinite worth"
in God's eyes. If, instead, the student had taken him
seriously about the sordid, dissolute, meaningless, and
worthless lifestyle that he was possibly trying to
confess, he would have been on the right track and
might have said, "You probably have some good
reasons for having reached that conclusion about
yourself. Tell me about them." If William then responded by doing so, at length the student might have
said, "William, you're right. That way of living—doing
your own thing while ignoring God and breaking all
His laws—in the end doesn't amount to much. No
wonder you've decided that you are 'nothin'.' That
kind of life is not only nothin', but it is a life of positive
harm. You have broken God's laws, dishonored His
name, hurt others around you, and destroyed yourself. In the Bible God calls you His 'enemy.' And yet,
in spite of all that, you can be saved from the punishment you deserve in hell. Let me tell you about a Savior
who, in spite of your sin and worthlessness, died
for people just like you. He can give you an entirely
different kind of life that will, in time, amount to
something. . . ."

One writer claims:

I am special because I exist. I have self-

worth . . . and no matter what I do I will never
lose this.[2]

If this is true, then not only Hitler, or criminals in
prison, but men and women suffering in hell must also
have a right to a good self-image! If the right to feel
good about one's self comes as part and parcel of mere
existence, then there is no place for guilt or loathing;
indeed, there is no need for repentance. We are all
entitled to self-worth, no matter what we do, simply
because God made us.

While speaking of criminals, you might think that
they are principally persons suffering from a sense of
low self-esteem. Not according to Yochelson and
Samenow, two doctors at St. Elizabeth's Hospital who
studied 200-plus criminals. They discovered that of the
lot there was not a single criminal "who believed he
was evil. Each criminal thought of himself as a basically good person . . . even when planning a crime."[3]
So the student was mistaken when he thought that this
man needed strokes. If William was not merely trying
to elicit pity, then the student might have had on his
hands a prisoner who was speaking to a religious
person out of guilt, wanting from him the message of
forgiveness and salvation rather than the false reassurance that amounted to saying he was okay in God's
eyes! If William wanted pity, the student's agreement
and invitation to talk about how bad he is would have
stopped him cold. Either way, taking him seriously
about his negative statements concerning himself
rather than telling him how good and valuable he is
would have been the biblical way to go, thereby giving
him a chance to meet a Savior who loves us and can

redeem us even in our lowly, fallen state.

Now let's look at some more verses calculated to reduce self-esteem. They tell us of man's innate wickedness from birth:

> Do you indeed speak righteousness, O gods?
> Do you judge uprightly, O sons of men? No,
> in heart you work unrighteousness; on earth
> you weigh out the violence of your hands.
> The wicked are estranged from the womb;
> these who speak lies go astray from birth.
> They have venom like the venom of a serpent;
> like a deaf cobra that stops up its ear, so that
> it does not hear the voice of charmers, or a
> skillful caster of spells (Psalm 58:1-5).

> Behold, I was brought forth in iniquity, and
> in sin my mother conceived me (Psalm 51:5).

In Psalm 62:9, God's Word weighs man in the scale and concludes:

> Men of low degree are only vanity, and men
> of rank are a lie; in the balances they go up;
> they are together lighter than breath.

What an astounding statement this is! Weighed by *God*, on *His* scales, man has no weight; indeed, throw all men together in a heap on the balance, and instead of weighing it down, God says that it will go up! They are like negative weight—lighter than nothing. What a graphic picture of man's utter nothingness!

According to the self-esteem teachings that we have

been investigating, man should have weighed heavily—perhaps he should have been of *infinite* weight! But God's Word declares that he is lighter than nothing—lighter than an empty scale.

In Psalm 8 the psalmist expresses his utter amazement that God "visits" (i.e., "looks after, cares for") man. "What is man?" he asks. In Psalm 62 we have the answer: nothing; less than nothing. It is not because of man's great value to God that He cares for him, but in spite of his lowliness. *That* is why the psalmist is amazed. This care shows something of *God's* greatness—not man's.

In His amazing grace and undeserved love, God cares for man. The great fact is that the Scriptures everywhere point us to the grace of God and not to the worth of man.

10

What Does the Bible Teach?

So far in this book I have tried to do two things: 1) I have tried to give you a fair picture of the self-esteem movement and its claims, and 2) I have evaluated it biblically and shown that, weighed in God's balance, it is found wanting. You might think that the book should end at this point, having come to a natural conclusion. However, if I left you here, all that I have done so far would be in vain. It is not enough to burn down a house; it is also necessary to erect another in its place. That I shall now attempt to do.

What is the biblical alternative to the self-worth approach? In an earlier chapter I discussed Matthew 6, in which Jesus Himself set forth two contrasting ways of life: the pagan way and the Christian way. The pagan way had as its priority becoming secure and significant through the accumulation of "things" to meet "needs." The Christian way puts God and His empire first. But how? What makes the difference?

Jesus sets forth self-denial rather than self-affirmation as the way to enter into a proper relationship with God. Seldom do we read in self-worth literature about self-denial, the one emphasis on self that *does* run all through the New Testament. We shall take a look at some of the key passages relating to this biblical emphasis and try to understand what God says, relating it all the while to the self-worth approach.

In 2 Timothy 3:2 we read of "lovers of self" (*philautoi*). Here this word is listed along with a host of other sinful aberrations that Timothy will have to avoid during the days of his forthcoming ministry. Paul's warning is timely to ministers today. Presumably there is a kind of self-love that is clearly condemned in the Scriptures. Since the word *philautoi* occurs only in 2 Timothy 3:2, in a list, without further explanation, we cannot discover anything about its exact meaning from the context. All we can say is that it keeps bad company with such characters as "blasphemers, slanderers, arrogant, and those who are pleasure-centered." Thoughtful consideration of the list in 2 Timothy 3 will lead you to the conclusion that every one of the items in it (and it is much longer than I have indicated here) could be said either to have a self-centered focus or to grow out of such a focus. It is easy to see the dangers of self-centeredness by studying it. And it should grieve us to think of children in Grand Rapids or elsewhere being encouraged to think they deserve a "pat on the back" and being told to "feel good" about themselves, thereby being led in the very pathway to selfishness that God condemns. Many of the problems listed in 2 Timothy 3 could appear in their lives later on as a result of encouraging, rather than curbing, the sinful tendencies that are inherent in fallen human nature (cf. Proverbs 22:15).

The proper thing to encourage, according to the Word of God, is self-denial. The command to deny self occurs six times explicitly in the Gospels, but the concept is everywhere in Scripture. That is what the Lord was getting at when He told His disciples to forget their own interests and put His affairs first ("seek first the kingdom of God and His righteousness").

What does God say about self? He says, "Deny self":

> Jesus said to His disciples, "If anyone wishes to come after Me, let him deny himself, and take up his cross, and follow Me. For whoever wishes to save his life will lose it; but whoever loses his life for My sake shall find it" (Matthew 16:24,25).

This does not mean that a person must deny himself some particular thing, as some erroneously suppose ("I'll give up chewing gum for Lent"), but it means to deny *one's own self* (literally "to say no to yourself"). If anything could stand in sharper contrast to Christ's command to deny self than the self-affirming, self-gratifying emphasis that we have been reading about in the self-esteem literature, I don't know what it is.

Just as Jesus set the Gentile way over against the Christian way of life in Matthew 6, here too He contrasts two utterly diverse and irreconcilable paths. The interesting fact that should not be missed is Jesus' antithetical way of stating this matter: There is no room for compromise. Quite the opposite of the eclectic integrationists, who want to merge and blend as much

of what the world has to say with biblical teachings
as they can, Jesus distances Himself from the pagan way
of life (Matthew 6) and from those who do not deny
self and follow Him but instead want to "save their
lives." This antithesis occurs in each of the Gospel
accounts (Mark 8:34-38; Luke 9:23-25; John 12:25).
Jesus says, "Whoever wishes to save his life shall lose
it; but whoever loses his life for My sake shall find it"
(Matthew 16:25). It is difficult to see how the integrationists can reckon with this.

The words translated "self" and "life" (*heauton* and
psuche) both mean "self" and refer to the same thing.
As a matter of fact, they are used interchangeably.
(Cf. Matthew 16:26 with Luke 9:25. In Matthew *psuche*
is used, whereas in Luke it is *heauton*.) Christ is telling
us not only to say no to ourselves and yes to Him
("follow Me"), but He affirms that we must put self
to death by "taking up our cross" (Luke adds "daily").
To take up the cross does not mean making some
particular sacrifice, nor does it refer to some particular burden ("My husband is my cross"). Anyone in that
day, reading those words, would know plainly that
taking up the cross meant one and only one thing:
putting to death an infamous criminal. Jesus, therefore,
is saying, "You must treat yourself, with all your sinful
ways, priorities, and desires, like a criminal, and put
self to death every day." That says something about
the self-image that Christ expects us to have!

That is bitter medicine for all of us, and especially
for self-worth proponents. Yet it is the only cure for
a church that increasingly is growing sick—of it*self*.
The seeming paradox is that the person who focuses
attention on himself will lose all he wants to preserve

for himself, whereas the person who puts Christ
and His interests first is the one who gains all that the
other loses. This is the same truth that Jesus taught
in Matthew 6. There the Gentiles zealously seek with
care and worry (and never really find satisfaction
in) the things that the Christian, who forgets about
his "needs" and puts Christ first, finds "added" to him.

In John 12:25 we read that "he who loves his life
[self] loses it; and he who hates his life [self] in this
world shall keep it to life eternal." Here there is a
strong warning. Indeed, the promotion of self-love is
the very thing warned against: "Whoever loves self. . .
loses it." Rather than love self, Christ says, in this
world we should lose self, or, as He puts it here, "hate
it," in order to preserve it for eternity. The two words
"lose" and "hate" mean virtually the same thing and
help interpret each other. They mean putting aside
one's own desires, interests, and concerns (even legitimate ones) in order to do Christ's bidding. "Hating"
self means "to love less," as it plainly does in Luke
14:26: "If anybody comes to Me, and does not hate
his own father and mother and wife and children and
brothers and sisters, yes, and even his own life, he
cannot be My disciple." We know that the word
"hate" in all these passages has such a meaning from
the parallel phrase in Matthew 10:37, where instead
of "hate" we read, "He who loves father or mother
more than Me is not worthy of Me; and he who loves
son or daughter *more than* Me is not worthy of Me."
To "hate" another person or one's own self is the same
as to put Christ and His kingdom before others or self.

This matter of denying self is not a peripheral issue.
It strikes hard at the core of self-worth, self-esteem,

self-love thinking. In self-love teaching the idea is not
merely that Christ and self can both be put on the same
level of priority (from Jesus' words it is clear that even
this is impossible; He calls on us to *choose* between
the two), but that before we can love and serve Christ
we must first be served and loved, and love ourselves.
Could any teaching be more plainly opposed to what
Jesus said?

The consequences of self-love dogma are very serious. These words of Jesus warn of eternal deprivation.
One wonders how many young people will be led
astray, led away from discipleship for Christ, which
requires losing their "selves," because they were told
"Feel good about yourself" rather than being told that
there is a criminal inside who needs to be put to death
daily. The danger is obvious in the words of the
psychologist who countered the words of his client,
telling her that "putting a priority on self-acceptance
is the first step many of us need to take" rather than
seeking first the kingdom of God.

God wants us to "lose" our selves in this world by
throwing ourselves wholeheartedly into the service
and love of Christ and His empire. Having children act
out a skit, "A Pat on the Back," and encouraging them
to write essays on what they like about themselves,
are activities that throw all the attention on self. Such
a wrong emphasis could be devastating to Christian
education.[1]

Let me say one more word about the passage in Luke
14:25-27. Discipleship, the subject in view in all the
passages that we have been studying in this chapter,
means the renunciation of all ties—even the closest and
dearest ones in life. It does not always mean that we

must forsake all others in order to follow Christ, but it *does* mean that we must have such allegiance to Him that we are ready at all times, if called upon, to do so. Jesus especially points out, as if this were the hardest part of all to do, that the disciple must renounce "even his own life (self) too." The great thing to which to point people is pleasing Christ, following Him, and doing His will. That will not confuse children—or others—or lead them astray! Anyone, including self, that gets in the way of that is wrong.

There can be no doubt about the fact that Christ was concerned about the self; it is not as though He ignored the subject. Indeed, He thought it of such importance that He spoke about it in the closest possible connection to discipleship and made definitive pronouncements about it. Yet in all this He gave no indication of man's great worth, nor did He allow any place for extenuating circumstances: "You can renounce all your ties and follow me after all your needs have been met and you have learned to love yourself." The very idea sounds ludicrous when you put it in Jesus' mouth!

And of course there are also other passages that speak of putting Christ before self. Take, for example, 2 Corinthians 5:15:

> He died for all, that they who live should no longer live for themselves but for Him who died and rose again on their behalf.

There you have it: One must no longer live for self, as he did before coming to Christ. The old way of life was put off in Christ, and now must be put off in our lives. The focus of life must now be "For me to live

is Christ" even though it once was "For me to live is
self." What could be clearer?

Now consider Romans 14:7,8:

> Not one of us lives for himself, and not one
> of us dies for himself; for if we live, we live
> for the Lord, or if we die, we die for the Lord;
> therefore whether we live or die, we are the
> Lord's.

Again, the main point of the passage is that Christ
is to take the place of self in the Christian's life. It is
not that this happens in any substantive sense, of
course, but in terms of desires and will and the like.
Eating and regarding days (v. 6) is not a private matter;
it affects other people, including new converts. No
Christian is to live out of regard for himself. "What
is for the welfare of the kingdom and for the honor
of Christ?" is the kind of question he should ask himself. His answer ought to be, "I shall live in such a way
that, whenever there is a choice, I shall gladly serve
Christ and others first." He must live for Christ, and,
as Paul says, if need be, die for Him.

Interestingly, the last part of verse 7 speaks cogently
to the suicide issue: "Not one of us dies [i.e., if he dies
properly] *for himself.*" Liddon says those words
mean—

> To welcome or seek death as a relief from the
> troubles of this life. Of this selfishness in
> death, suicide is the highest expression.[2]

Liddon's words are important. Paul's whole point

is that we must not do anything—live or die—for ourselves; all must be done for Christ. A suicide dies for himself; no suicide could die for Christ. It is because of this verse that we know that suicide is an act of the old man, of self-centered thinking, which at times (among the Stoics and some modern existentialists) has even been encouraged.

Holliday, who shot himself, and Wanda Williams, who hanged herself, both committed selfish acts of self-murder. They thought nothing of loved ones, or students, or anyone else. They were thinking of themselves as indeed their suicide notes indicate. It was not low self-esteem that did them in, but too high a regard for self. They said, in effect, "I am too good to be treated this way. I will put up with it no longer."

The Scriptures teach us that Christians own nothing, not even their lives, since Christ has purchased them. The minute you get that fact wrong, and think that anything, even your own self, is really yours, you don't own it—it owns you!

Love itself is the very cessation of self-directed, self-concerned, self-centered living. That's why living for Christ and others out of love for them points us away from ourselves. Self-esteem pursuits deflect one's attention from others and thus destroy Christian love. Rather than laying the groundwork for love (layers upon which to build it, as the Adler/Maslow scheme says), it erodes everything worthwhile. Love—other-directed concern—alone sets us free from self.

Contrary to the modern emphasis we have been studying, the Bible teaches that you can't properly relate to yourself ("find" or "save" self) until you learn to love others. As usual, pagan thinking reverses

God's order of things.

Jesus disposed of the myth that we can love others only after they have first loved us by saying,

> If you love those who love you, what credit
> is that to you? For even sinners love those
> who love them (Luke 6:32).

In effect, by referring to "sinners" (i.e., enemies of God), He characterized, once and for all, the "I'll love you if you first love me" position as ungodly.

For a Christian, the alternative to self-love, self-esteem, self-worth, and any other kind of self-centered teaching that might appear in the future is clearly self-denial. When you seek to gain yourself, you can only lose it; when you are willing to lose yourself for Christ, you save it. It's that simple—and that profound.

An Accurate Self-Image

11

While there is no concern evidenced in the Bible about people having too little self-esteem, and therefore no directions for enhancing self-esteem, God does indicate that He wants us to evaluate ourselves—so far as it is possible to do so—*accurately*. This point was made tellingly some years ago by my colleague John Bettler, the Director of the Christian Counseling and Educational Foundation, Laverock, Pennsylvania.

This command, to make an honest evaluation of yourself, emerges preeminently in Romans 12:3:

> Through the grace given to me I say to every man among you not to think more highly of himself than he ought to think, but to think so as to have sound judgment, as God has allotted to each a measure of faith.

Following this exhortation, Paul goes on to speak

of the varying gifts and responsibilities that God has given to each member of His church. Self-evaluation has to do largely with such matters: how well we are exercising those gifts. But notice the principle of evaluation: The words "sound judgment" mean (and demand) that a reasoned judgment, based on evidence, must be made. The verse also clearly indicates that all people are not to make the same judgment about themselves merely because they exist as creatures or even redeemed children of God, bearing His image. Each must make his own evaluation of himself according to the evidence.

Literally, the operative part of the verse reads:

> . . .not to be high-minded above that which
> he ought to be minded, but to be so minded
> as to be sober-minded.

As you can see from this literal rendering, there is a play on the word "minded" and its derivatives that runs through this portion of the verse. All of these words have to do with *reasoned* evaluation of *evidence*.

Don't fail to notice that in warning against faulty evaluation, Paul says nothing about the possibility of underevaluating one's self. That is not a likely possibility. His only warning is against making too high an estimate: "Don't think *more highly* of yourself than you ought to." The Holy Spirit, writing through Paul, knows us very well!

Consider this:

> Each year the College Board invites the mil-
> lion high school seniors who take its aptitude

test to indicate various things about themselves, including "How you feel you compare
with other people your own age in certain
areas of ability." Judging from their responses
in the most recent year for which data are
available, it appears that America's high
school students are not racked with "a sense
of low self-esteem."

In "leadership ability," 70 percent rated
themselves above average, 2 percent below
average. Sixty percent view themselves as
better than average in "athletic ability," and
only 6 percent as below average. In "ability
to get along with others," *zero* percent of
the 829,000 students who responded rated
themselves below average, 60 percent rated
themselves in the top 10 percent, and 25
percent see themselves among the top 1
percent.[1]

Consider also:

In one study, 94 percent of college faculty
think themselves better than their average
colleague.[2]

You would think that the words of this verse would
give self-esteem advocates some pause. But, thinking
more highly of their dogma than they ought to, this
verse becomes for them just another "integrate" into
the system.

In a pamphlet *The Healing of the Mind*, the unnamed author, commenting on Romans 12:3, says:

> This admonition does not encourage a low estimation, but a true one.

Right so far. But now watch the subtle next step in his argument:

> It actually indicates he is to think highly of himself.

Not so. Probably he is thinking of the English translation "more highly." It is true that such wording might indicate that it is all right to think highly, so long as you don't think *too* highly. (But even that translation doesn't say that a person ought to think highly; it would merely permit it if legitimate.) But remember what the more literal translation says—that a person is not "to be high-minded above that which you are to be minded." That changes the tone of the verse altogether. There is a warning against high-mindedness —nothing more. When anyone is high-minded, he is minded above that which he ought to be minded. All high-mindedness is wrong. Because the verse does not permit high-mindedness at all, it speaks against most of the self-worth literature.

Paul is concerned about the all-too-common tendency of believers to think too highly of themselves. Hosea 7:9 points out this frequently occurring fault among God's people, using a graphic illustration:

> Strangers devour his strength, yet he does not

know it; gray hairs also are sprinkled on him,
yet he does not know it.

The tribe of Ephraim is pictured as a man who thinks
he is stronger than he actually is. His self-evaluation
is too high, and he will discover that fact the hard
way.

Because what we think of our gifts, and how well
we are using them, is important to our service for
Christ, we *must* evaluate them *soberly*, according to
actual evidence. That is why Paul, in telling us how
to evaluate ourselves, warns:

If anyone thinks he is something when he is
nothing, he deceives himself (Galatians 6:3).

Stop a moment and reflect on the words "something" and "nothing." Could a proponent of the self-
esteem view ever bring himself to call someone a
"nothing"? Yet Paul did so more than once (remember 1 Corinthians 13). Remember that Paul's words
reveal God's estimate of Christians who are failing to
live as they should!

Many people who are accepting the self-esteem
teachings not only "deceive" themselves by thinking that they are something when they are nothing
(that's bad enough), but they exult over it and teach
God's little ones to do the same. It is to keep people
from exulting over how good they are that Paul
wrote these words. His whole point was that we
ought not to compare ourselves with others when
evaluating:

> Let each one examine his own work, and then
> he will have reason for boasting in regard to
> himself alone, and not in regard to another
> (Galatians 6:4).

A sober evaluation is made not on the basis of how
well one is doing in comparison with others, but by
comparing one's work with scriptural standards. If we
come out well on that score—and how often do we?—
we will have solid reasons for satisfaction.

Nowhere does he say that we should feel good about
ourselves because we exist, because we were made in
the image of God, or even because, in Christ, we are
made perfect *in God's sight*. Rather, because of our
sinful tendency to find other people with whom it is
easy to compare ourselves favorably (instead of basing our judgment upon genuine achievement), Paul
warned against all such self-deception. He instructed
the Galatians that if a brother tries to restore another
while holding a false opinion of himself, he will fail
and probably do more harm than good, since he
himself is liable to get caught in the same sin. Let him
who thinks he stands take heed lest he fall.

Nor is a sinner able to think soberly about himself
by reflecting on himself alone.[3] Paul does not say
to do that. A Christian can think soberly only by
measuring his work—real, tangible achievements—
against the biblical standard.

Whenever we talk about "worth" and "value," we
talk in the air unless we have a standard of value against
which to evaluate.

To sum up what we have seen so far, and put it in
a form in which we can compare and contrast it with

the teaching of the self-esteem proponents, note the
following:

1. It must not be the Christian's concern to
   pursue self-worth, but rather to become a
   worthy self.
2. Satisfaction, like peace and joy, comes not
   when one pursues it, but unexpectedly
   and always as a by-product of faithful,
   fruitful Christian living. The Christian
   evaluates achievement according to the
   standards of the Bible—achievement ef-
   fected by grace—and not by one's own
   unaided self-efforts.
3. The self-worth position teaches that regardless of how he behaves, a person has
   a right to love himself and in fact ought
   to like himself; until he does, he may never
   change his behavior.
4. Self-esteem thinkers even teach that sin
   is due to low self-esteem,[4] whereas God
   teaches that it is due to one's sinful nature.

In self-evaluation, therefore, standards differing
widely from biblical standards of judgment prevail.

Real Life

"All right, theoretically you may have convinced me, but what about the result of all this in real life? What would you do with Midge, for example, and what about children that are continually denegraded by parents and other people? You've got to say something about this kind of thing before you finish this book or you will surely leave me dissatisfied."

You are entitled to have a look at some real-life cases. Turn back to the case of Midge, to start with (Chapter 3). If you sum up all that she says, here is what it amounts to: "My problems are due to the way that others, including God, have treated me. If people were only nicer to me and more considerate and understanding of me, I'd be happy." Midge is wrong. And so long as she goes on thinking that way, and acting in accordance with it, she will continue to be miserable—and miserable to be with.

Midge needs to be shown, biblically, that peace and

joy come not from others but from God: "The kingdom of God is not eating and drinking, but righteousness and peace and joy in the Holy Spirit" (Romans
14:17). "May the God of hope fill you with all joy and
peace in believing, that you may abound in hope by
the power of the Holy Spirit" (Romans 15:13). If she
does not have peace and joy, and is truly a Christian,
then her relationship to God has gone sour (a fact
which is evident from the case itself). She must be
brought to repentance over the bitterness that she
holds against other people and against God Himself.
Because she attributes her problems to a poor self-
image, she feels helpless; when she comes to see that
she *deserves* a poor self-image because of the poor self
that she has become, she will be on the right track.
Instead of passively sitting around, waiting for others
to satisfy her "needs" at lower levels so that she can
become the sort of outgoing person she ought to be,
she must be made aware of the fact that she can reach
out to others *now*, developing friendships out of
serving others and showing love to them. As she begins
to do so, the situation will change. But she must be
warned that she must not change her behavior simply
as a gimmick to get a husband or to feel better; she
must do so because Christ wants her to and because
she wants to please Him out of gratitude for what He
has done for her. When she truly puts Christ and His
kingdom first, she will develop into a more attractive
and happier person as a by-product.

Now back to criminals, the State of California, and
the study by Yochelson and Samenow. Listen to this
letter to the editor that appeared in *U.S. News and
World Report*, April 15, 1985, written by a boy who

murdered his mother. Such criminals, we are being
told, are persons with low self-esteem brought on by
the abuse and browbeating of other people who continually put them down. Clearly this wasn't his problem, as you will see for yourself. Probably, as the tone
and purpose of the letter indicate, he was writing out
of a very high sense of self-esteem. Referring to an
article in which he was mentioned in an earlier issue
of the magazine, he writes:

> I am the boy who killed his mother. I need
> to write for two reasons: One, as part of this
> "culture" I feel I can relate; and, two, to set
> the record straight about my case.

> I disagree with people who say that parents
> are to blame. It was not my mom's fault that
> I was the way I was, and it certainly wasn't
> her fault that I murdered her. The article says
> that my mother "ignored me until the pres-
> sure blew me up." This was the impression
> I gave to people involved in my case. It is not
> true. I received no unfair treatment, nor did
> I have to go through anything that other kids
> don't go through as a part of growing up. Kids
> have gone through it for centuries.

> The real problem was how I chose to deal
> with what did happen. I am not saying that
> things don't happen to cause kids to do
> things. In my situation, I am the only one to
> be blamed for what I did and for the immense
> pain I caused many people. I really need to

> make that clear. I lied in the beginning due
> to my own selfishness. I lied so that I would
> not have to honestly look at who I was and
> what I had done.

In those words you have the principal points he
made. Two things stand out: 1) This boy knew all
along what the real problem was—himself. He was
knowledgeable about self-esteem views at least to some
extent and used that knowledge to deceive those who
interviewed him for a previous article, and attempted
to get off the hook by using it with the authorities.
2) He puts the finger squarely on the real problem: "I
choose. . .I am the only one to be blamed." That is
right. He says, "So what if I had troubles at home? Kids
have been having trouble with their parents ignoring
them, putting them down, etc., for centuries. That
doesn't make them do what they do. They *choose* to
become murderers, etc., when they could have gone
some other way." Again, he is right. Putting people
down doesn't cause them to do anything; they must
decide to do whatever they do in response.

Let me say that the State of California (and all others
who want to use our hard-earned tax money on studies
designed to stop criminality through raising the self-
worth of potential criminals) might profit from studying the results of the Yochelson/Samenow report of
work with 200-plus criminals over a 15-year period.
Here are some of their conclusions. For the first five
years, according to Yochelson—

> Using traditional methods, the criminals made
> fools of us . . . . They . . . exploited us for their

own purposes. . . . They became criminals
with insight into their past, but criminals
nonetheless. . . insight gave them more material to excuse their behavior.

So they changed their tactics:

Instead of trying to allay feelings of guilt. . .
they tried to bring out and sustain the criminal's disgust with himself. They attempted to
"indicate to him just how rotten a person
he was". . . and "voiced contempt while
indicating a willingness to work with the
criminal."[1]

Only then did they begin to get results. As I mentioned before, they "never found a criminal who
believed he was evil. Each criminal thought of himself
as a basically good person." Even in criminals, self-
esteem is strong. Indeed, it was so high in these 200
or so criminals that the only way to reach them was
to batter it down. Even the problem of the criminal
is not low self-esteem; he thinks of himself as a good
person because sinful human nature, acting like the
lawyer to whom Christ told the story of the Good
Samaritan, justifies itself. People talk themselves into
thinking that they are good, just as that atheist in Psalm
14 talks himself into thinking that there is no God.

"All right. I'll buy what you say about criminals and
even about teenage criminal types, but what about little
children? There certainly does seem to be something
to the self-worth argument that if you put down a little
child, he will grow up with a bad self-concept and that

this in turn will hurt him throughout life.''

No, human beings are human beings. While the child is different from the adult in many ways, the dynamic about which we are thinking is no different in children than in adults. That is because children are born with a sinful nature, and so start life self-centered. The self-worth enthusiasts make much of denigration of children. They call it "verbal child abuse" and denounce all parents who speak harshly to their children or ever put them down. While sinful parents do treat their children poorly at times, is the result so devastating as the self-worth people think? Listen to what some of them are saying. Speaking of a child who was "verbally abused," one famous Christian psychologist wrote:

> But you can bet he heard his mother, and his self-concept will *always* [emphasis his] reflect what she said.[2]

Elsewhere in the same book, regarding another child, he says:

> Her self-concept will never recover from the nightmares he inflicted on her tender mind.[3]

If he is right, and rough handling of these tender plants will so affect their self-concept that they will "always" reflect this and "never recover" from it, then the matter certainly must be serious. Surely the parent was wrong and undoubtedly has caused his child to face serious problems, but using such categorical words as "always" and "never" makes it seem that the damage is irreparable. What is easily forgotten is what the teenage murderer so well pointed out: Children have been going through this sort of thing for years. They must not be so tender after all. What about all the kids who grew up for centuries before the self-image people began to work on parents? How did they make it? How did pagans, growing up in homes where infanticide and all kinds of other gruesome things went on, ever "recover" to become sterling Christians after conversion? Something must be wrong here. Something *is* wrong!

Listen to another Christian psychologist:

> Our sense of belongingness is fundamentally established in infancy. . . . The underlying sense of worthiness developed in childhood does not seem to change because one is criticized or praised.

But is it really true that we are stuck with what was done to us in infancy and childhood, and that nothing can be done about it? There is something wrong here; surely the gospel and the power of Christ can change a person. Is a mother's poor handling of her child so indelible that even the power of the Holy Spirit cannot erase it?

The writer goes on to say:

> The first year is fundamental to developing a sense of being somebody or of being nobody, and these basic feelings can last a lifetime.[4]

Here, at least, he does not insist that they *will* last a lifetime. Permit me to quote one more:

> The roots of his trouble probably lie in child-
> hood experiences which have left an indelible
> mark on his personality, or in certain religious
> presuppositions which have been drilled into
> him and which he cannot shake off.

The author is speaking of a grown Christian man. Is there hope? He is not sure:

> It is also possible that a person with problems
> as deep-seated as these will never be able to
> attain a consistently positive self-image.[5]

These statements, only representative of many like them, indicate that self-image thinkers believe children are largely, if not totally, stuck with what happens to them in the earliest years. But a fundamental teaching of our Christian faith is that we are freed from the dominion of our past by Christ and are able to serve Him faithfully and fully if only we are willing to (cf. Romans 6; 1 Corinthians 6).

Listen to 1 Peter 1:18,19:

> You were not redeemed with perishable
> things like silver or gold from your futile way
> of life inherited from your forefathers (verse
> 18),

> but with precious blood, as of a lamb un-
> blemished and spotless, the blood of Christ
> (verse 19).

Many Corinthians and Thessalonians who became believers, capable of showing so great love that it was spoken about all over the Mediterranean world (1 Thessalonians 1:6-10), were maltreated in youth, in pagan homes where not even the slightest thought was given to preserving and building a good self-image. The New Testament writers expected their readers to serve Christ, loving God and neighbor, regardless of what happened to them as children and youth.

How can this be? Can a child understand all this? What happens to a little child when he is maltreated by an adult? To begin with, please understand that I am certainly not justifying parents for manhandling children; for them to do so is reprehensible and must be condemned. Even verbal abuse, which can be every bit as painful to a child as physical abuse, ought not to occur in homes. But this is not to say that there is no remedy for any ill effects that may occur. That is the point I wish to make.

What happens, then? First, every baby is born a sinner. Many Scriptures, such as Psalm 51:5, etc., make this clear. And, although the self-image people fail to reckon with this, little sinners sin; it is not only their parents who do so. They do wrong themselves, and *they respond sinfully to sinful treatment from parents or other people.* This is the crucial point to keep in mind. They learn to speak ill of those who speak ill of them. Their wrong responses may include wrong patterns of thinking about themselves. They may accept false ideas about themselves that parents or others say ("You have no ability.") In other words, being little sinners, they will in all likelihood fail to make the reasonable evaluation of themselves that Paul commands in Romans 12:3. And, in addition to their own sinful responses to the erroneous ideas that other people impart, they also copy the sinful patterns (even thought patterns) expressed by adults (1 Peter 1:18).

It is true that adult sinners, by their inconsiderateness and thoughtless words, tempt little sinners to sin by providing poor models, by telling them wrong things (often about themselves), and by abusing them verbally or physically. But in all this, *what children do wrong in response to sin is also sin.* This must never be forgotten because it is where the hope lies. What must be rejected is the notion that their parents and others *directly and irreversibly* affect them for life by the wrong they do to them. Such a teaching is too simplistic. In reality, what happens is a two-step process. The adult wrongs the child, then the child or younger person in response sins (and perhaps eventually even develops a sinful response pattern). But because this is the dynamic involved, there is hope. The hope is that in Christ not only can their sins be forgiven, but the sinful patterns and even the sinful ways of thinking about themselves can be changed.

"How do you know that there is hope for change? How do you know that it is not inherent in human nature that a person can be affected adversely for life by what others say and do to him?" Here is how: Jesus was born a little nonsinner. That fact makes everything crystal clear. If others could do permanent harm to Him by the way they treated Him, He would have grown up with problems like all of the rest are supposed to have. But, as you know, He was totally free from problems. That means that there is nothing in human nature itself that can be *directly* affected in an adverse way by other people. What becomes stamped on little sinners is not what others have done to them, but the patterns of response that they themselves develop and etch into their way of life. But, as we have seen in 1 Peter 1:18 and elsewhere, it is precisely such patterns that Christ is able to free us from. The hope lies in the marvelous fact that Christ came to deal with sin.

This thesis about Jesus as a child is borne out in the one incident that we have of Him in His youth: the time He was left in the temple by His parents. The event is recorded in Luke 2:40-52. There we see Jesus *misunderstood and mishandled by His parents, who in anger, fear, and concern wrongly accused and rebuked Him.* Yet as a little nonsinner He responded righteously. There you see how every child ought to respond to wrong. What did Jesus do and say?

As parents go, certainly Joseph and Mary must have been among the best. But they were sinners, and at a time of crisis like this, when fear and worry took over, their sin became apparent. They blamed Jesus when, as He pointed out, they themselves were at fault. They focused on self, when, as He observed, their concern should have been His Father's house, as His was.

When His parents, whose focus was on themselves, asked, "Why have You treated us this way?" (Luke 2:48), He refused to listen to their criticism of His actions. He knew that He had done no wrong and He was not to be intimidated (or injured) by the self-centered attitude in which they addressed these words to Him. Instead, here is His response: "Why is it that you were looking for me? Did you not know that I had to be in My Father's house?"

He refused to accept blame and respectfully told His parents that they were the ones who were wrong. He asked, "Why look all over the place as you did? If you had a problem finding me, that was your fault, not mine. Don't place the blame on me; place it squarely where it belongs. You should have known I would be in the temple, my Father's house. Where else would you expect to find me?" Notice that He answered back; He did not internalize the wrong and let it fester within Him. (Little sinners might do that.) He asked question for question. He said that they were wrong or at best foolish for being upset. He did not buy their wrong view of the situation, thus troubling Himself within, but corrected it. He did not ask for forgiveness for wronging them, as Mary alleged. He did not go along with their self-pitying focus on themselves. He did not allow Himself to be embarrassed or "put down" by the rebuke He received. And He certainly didn't develop a bad or lower (even slightly lower) self-image as the result of their verbal wrong. He demonstrated an independence of thought that allowed Him to evaluate what was said and to reject what was wrong without any of that wrong affecting Him detrimentally in any way whatever. In short, He handled their wrongdoing rightly.

My concern here is to discover whether human nature *as such* is susceptible to such strong influence by other people that, against one's will, a person may be warped for life with problems and patterns of living that are inflicted upon him. The evidence is negative. Jesus, coming in sinless human nature, demonstrated that *without the cooperation of the one wronged*, the wrongdoing will *not* influence the one wronged.

Were little sinners instead little nonsinners just like Jesus, they too would respond properly. But the great fact is that the problem is not in human nature *as such*—that it is so impressionable that all wrongs done will inevitably produce lasting, indelible effects. Rather, the problem is that we have a sinful nature that will always tend toward sin. But when we grow up and come to Christ, all the sinful patterns we developed can be replaced by righteous ones. This is because the process of developing a life pattern (or habit) is a two-step one: 1) Wrong is done; 2) a wrong response is made. Because the wrong response is the act of the one who is sinned against, and not something done *to* him (in which he has no responsibility), there is the possibility for change. Of course, that is just what sanctification is all about; it is an ongoing process that gradually restores human nature to what it should be.

There is every reason for rejecting self-esteem views.

To summarize, we may say that the proponents of these views unwittingly:

1. exalt man when God ought to be exalted;
2. promote a humanistic way of life instead of the biblical, God-centered one;
3. frustrate believers who seek to love God and neighbor by telling them they cannot do so until others properly love them and they come to love themselves first;
4. advocate impossible standards of child-training and place unbearable burdens on parents' backs;
5. take away hope by suggesting that wrong treatment develops self-image problems

that may be life-lasting and beyond the
reach of the work of the Holy Spirit;

6. direct people into paths of self-pity and
   selfishness;

7. deny grace by basing salvation on man's
   supposed worth and value to God;

8. contrary to Jesus' words set men on a
   course of seeking self when they should
   be denying self, thus leading them away
   from Christian discipleship.

I urge you to become more discriminating about
what you hear and read.

CONCLUSION

You have heard a rather full presentation of two
views. You cannot accept them both. You must choose
between them. Will you go the way of humanism, with
its hopelessness and despair? Or will you go the way
of Christ, with hope and expectation? The choice is
yours.

Whether you buy into the self-worth, self-esteem
philosophy is not merely an academic matter. The decision will have vast ramifications. Much is at stake. The
ability of the church to withstand the impact of humanism on other fronts is involved. The welfare of your
children may hang in the balance (remember Wanda!).
Your own capacity for serving God will be affected,
and, of greatest importance, whether you live for God
or self is at the very center of your decision.

I urge you, therefore, to abandon entirely the self-esteem message. That will not be easy because you will hear it on radio and from the pulpit; you will read it in newspapers, books, and magazines. It is everywhere.

You must be alert and become more and more discerning. Even those who may have much to say that is helpful may occasionally mix it with self-worth teaching. You must learn to distinguish the true from the false. When you do, you will find it possible to help others to also become more discerning. This book is an attempt to assist you in this endeavor. May the great God of Glory, who alone is "worthy . . . to receive glory and honor and power" . . . "equip you in every good thing to do His will, working in us that which is pleasing in His sight, through Jesus Christ, to whom be the glory forever and ever. Amen" (Revelation 4:11; Hebrews 13:21).

Epilogue

Now that you have read this book, I hope you are deeply concerned about the inroads of the New Reformation in the church—concerned enough to *do* something about it.

"But what can *I* do?" you ask.

Any number of things. Let me suggest just a few.

First, you can do all you can to resist the entrance of self-esteem teaching into your congregation. You can do this by distributing informative literature to key people, by calling attention to self-esteem propaganda in materials used in the congregation, and by speaking to those who teach or promote self-worth thinking in Sunday school classes or elsewhere. All of this should be done in a loving, informative manner; avoid any and all divisiveness.

Second, you can write to publishers of books and magazines who promote self-esteem teaching, urging them to rethink their position. You can write to TV and radio preachers who have fallen for its tenets, pointing out its errors and sending helpful literature that counters these errors.

Third, you can pray for key leaders in the church who have become enamored with self-esteem thought and practice.

Fourth, you can find out what position your local Christian school takes on the self-worth question and whether such teaching underlies their educational practices and policies in instructing and relating to your children. Talk to administrators, teachers, and board members about the matter.

Fifth, you can strategically place books exposing and refuting the self-esteem movement in the hands of Christian leaders. You can donate copies to churches and Christian school libraries and generally encourage Christians to read such materials.

Last, you can deliver brief (or longer) talks on the subject, encourage discussions about it at church, or give book reports concerning the problem.

Doubtless there are many other ways to confront the New Reformation. Be creative, but also be kind. Most Christians lack discernment; they need instruction and help before rebuke. Give it to them. Don't turn them off. But also be clear, firm, and lovingly persistent. Point out the dangers: the demand of the new information for wholesale changes in methods and message, and the pervasive nature of self-worth thought.

Only if Christians like you become concerned to do more than shake their heads over what is happening can we turn the tide. Don't just put this book aside; determine right now at least one thing that you *will* do. *Schedule it* and then *do it*. May God bless you as you step out. Through you and others like you may He preserve His church from this plague in our time.

NOTES

CHAPTER 1

1. Rod Mays, *The Counsel of Chalcendon,* Vol. VII, No. 1, 1985.
2. Robert H. Schuller, *Self-Esteem: The New Reformation* (Waco: (Word Books, 1982), p. 15.
3. Ibid., p. 19
4. James Dobson, *What Wives Wish Their Husbands Knew about Women* (Wheaton: Tyndale House, 1975), p. 35.
5. Barnett, Baruch, and Rivers, "The Secret of Self-Esteem," in *The Ladies Home Journal,* Feb. 1984, p. 54.
6. Ibid., p. 62.
7. Philip A. Captain, *Eight Stages of Christian Growth* (Englewood Cliffs: Prentice Hall, 1984).
8. Ibid., p. 40.
9. Walter Trobisch, *Love Yourself* (Downers Grove: Inter-Varsity Press, 1976), p. 33.
10. Robert S. Brinkerhoff, *Christian Home and School,* Mar. 1985.
11. James Dobson, *Hide or Seek* (Old Tappan: Fleming H. Revell Co., 1974), p. 80.
12. *Time,* Feb. 11, 1985.
13. Ibid.
14. John H. Miller, *Why We Act That Way* (Nashville: Abingdon, 1946), p. 37.
15. Arthur Rouner, *You Can Learn to Like Yourself* (Grand Rapids: Baker Book House, 1978), p. 3.
16. Maurice Wagner, *The Sensation of Being Somebody* (Grand Rapids: Zondervan, 1975), p. 123.
17. Miller, op. cit., p. 37.
18. Ray Burwick, *Self Esteem: You're Better Than You Think* (Wheaton: Tyndale House, 1983), p. 34.
19. Dobson, op. cit., p. 148.

CHAPTER 2

1. Anthony A. Hoekema, *The Christian Looks at Himself* (Grand Rapids: Eerdmans, 1975), p. 116.

2. Ibid., p. 122.
3. Donna Foster, *Building a Child's Self-Esteem* (Glendale: Regal Books, 1977), p. 8.
4. Ibid., p. 11.
5. Ibid., p. 23.
6. Hoekema, op. cit., p. 16.
7. Ibid., p. 17.
8. Schuller, op. cit., p. 98.
9. Ibid., p. 38.
10. Robert Schuller, in Craig Ellison, *Your Better Self* (San Francisco: Harper and Row, 1982), p. 194.
11. Ibid., p. 198.
12. Jeff Boer, "Is Self-Esteem Proper for a Christian?" in *The Journal of Pastoral Practice,* Vol. 5, No. 4, p. 78.
13. Horatius Bonar, *God's Way of Peace,* (Grand Rapids: Baker Book House, 1984), pp. 26-27.
14. Ibid., p. 27.
15. Wesner Fallaw, "Beyond Egoism," in *Religion and Human Behavior* (New York: Association Press, 1954), p. 171.
16. Ibid., p. 96.
17. H. Norman Wright, *Improving Your Self-Image* (Eugene: Harvest House, 1977), p. 9.

CHAPTER 3

1. Bruce Narramore, *You're Someone Special* (Grand Rapids: Zondervan, 1978), p. 22.
2. Ibid., p. 22.
3. Lawrence Crabb, *Effective Biblical Counseling* (Grand Rapids: Zondervan, 1977), p. 80.
4. Walter Trobisch, *Love Yourself* (Downers Grove: Inter-Varsity Press, 1976), p. 11.
5. Op. cit., p. 157.
6. J.W. Jepson, *Don't Blame It All on Adam* (Minneapolis: Bethany, 1984), p. 85.
7. Ibid., p. 86.
8. Ibid., p. 11.
9. Ibid., p. 23.
10. Narramore, op. cit., p. 167.
11. Jay Adams, *The Christian Counselor's Casebook* (Grand Rapids: Zondervan, 1986), p. 40.
12. Linda M. Rourke, "Encouraged," in *Decision*, Feb. 1985, p. 6.
13. James M. Hatch, *God's Blueprint for Biblical Parenting* (Columbia: Columbia Bible College, 1983), p. 48.

CHAPTER 4

1. Crabb, op. cit., p. 79.
2. Matthew 4:4.
3. Crabb, op. cit., p. 61.
4. Bruce Narramore, op. cit., p. 115.
5. Bonaro W. Overstreet, "The Unloving Personality and the Religion of Love," in Simon Doniger, *Religion and Human Behavior* (New York: Association Press, 1954), p. 75.
6. Ibid., p. 74.
7. Matthew 6:25-34.

Chapter 5

1. Fallaw, op. cit., p. 165.
2. Fallaw, op. cit., p. 164.
3. Ibid.
4. Dennis J. DeHaan, *Daily Bread,* Feb. 1985.
5. From Andre Bustanoby, *You Can Change Your Personality* (Grand Rapids: Zondervan, 1976), pp. 40-42.
6. Hedges and Betty Capers, in Herbert Otto, ed., *Marriage and Family Enrichment* (Nashville: Parthenon Press, 1976), p. 165.
7. Wm. H. Masters and Virginia E. Johnson, *The Pleasure Bond* (New York: Bantam Books, 1975), pp. 118, 152, 154, 156.
8. Of course there are nontechnical situations in which the word may be used in a more relaxed manner (particularly in its verbal forms: "I need a shovel to dig a hole"). But this semitechnical substitution of *need* for *desire* must always be avoided.
9. Jay Adams, *Matters of Concern to Christian Counselors* (Phillipsburg: Presbyterian and Reformed Publishing Co., 1978), pp. 41-42.
10. Crabb, op. cit., p. 81.

Chapter 6

1. Trobisch, op. cit., p. 11.
2. Ibid., p. 11.
3. Ibid.
4. Crabb, op. cit., p. 81.
5. Captain, op. cit.
6. Trobisch, op. cit., p. 11.

CHAPTER 7

1. Hoekema, op. cit., p. 45.
2. Robert Morey, *Death and the Afterlife* (Minneapolis: Bethany, 1985), p. 37.
3. Hoekema, op. cit., p. 22.
4. Narramore, op. cit., p. 23.
5. Morey, op. cit., p. 37.
6. Bruce Rathbun, a student at Westminster Theological Seminary in Philadelphia. Reported in *The Presbyterial Journal*, Apr. 24, 1985. Schuller's new evangelism-by-strokes has caught on widely. An evangelistic tract entitled "You're Special" reads "You are special indeed! The Bible reveals God's total interest in you as an individual. . . yes, you are valuable to God!" (Ted Griffin, Good News Publishers, n.d., #6C04.)
7. Schuller, *Self-Esteem,* op. cit., p. 151.
8. Rouner, Arthur, *You Can Learn to Like Yourself* (Grand Rapids: Baker Book House, 1978), p. 4.
9. Ibid., p. 5.
10. Dennis J. De Haan, op. cit.

CHAPTER 8

1. Wright, op. cit., p. 36.
2. William Kirwin, *Biblical Concepts for Christian Counseling* (Grand Rapids: Baker Book House, 1984), p. 107.
3. Foster, op. cit., p. 6.
4. J.E. Jones, *Reconciliation* (Minneapolis: Bethany, 1984), p. 139.
5. Dennis J. De Haan, *Our Daily Bread*, Feb. 26, 1985.
6. Jepson, op. cit., p. 85.
7. Burwick, op. cit., p. 80.
8. Morey, op. cit., p. 41.
9. J. I. Packer, *Keep in Step with the Spirit* (Old Tappan: Revell, 1984), p. 97.

CHAPTER 9

1. Op. cit., p. 17.
2. Captain, op. cit., p. 53.
3. Robert Pear, *The Washington Star,* Aug. 15, 1976.

CHAPTER 10

1. For information about a truly Christian school program, in which the emphasis is not on self but on ministry to others in Christ's name, see my *Back to the Blackboard*, (Presbyterian and Reformed Publishing Co., 1982).
2. H.P. Liddon, *Explanatory Analysis of St. Paul's Epistle to the Romans* (London: Longman's Green and Co., 1899), p. 262.

CHAPTER 11

1. David Meyers, *The Inflated Self* (New York: Seabury, 1981), pp. 23-24.
2. David Meyers, "A New Look at Pride," in *Your Better Self*, op. cit., p. 90.
3. Cf. especially Proverbs 16:2; 21:2. These verses indicate that one's self-image (how he looks to himself, or, as Proverbs puts it, "in his own eyes") is basically unsound. When we attempt self-evaluation, we tend not to rate ourselves too low, as the teachers of the New Reformation think, but too highly. Only God's evaluation of the heart is truly accurate.
4. Wagner, op. cit., p. 24.

CHAPTER 12

1. Pear, op. cit., Aug. 15, 1976.
2. Dobson, op. cit., p. 52.
3. Ibid, p. 81.
4. Wagner, op. cit., pp. 34, 35, 61.
5. Hoekema, op. cit., p. 94.